Wake Up in Bed, Together!

CLAUDE NOLTE, Ph.D. and DOROTHY NOLTE, Ph.D.

Wake Up in Bed, Together!

A HANDBOOK FOR SEXUAL REPATTERNING

STEIN AND DAY/*Publishers*/New York

First published in 1975
Copyright © 1974 by Claude and Dorothy Nolte
Library of Congress Catalog No. 74-81991
All rights reserved
Designed by David Miller
Printed in the United States of America
Stein and Day/*Publishers*/Scarborough House,
Briarcliff Manor, N. Y. 10510
ISBN 0-8128-1739-7

SECOND PRINTING 1976

To the memory of the late
Arnold Kegel, M.D., and his
life work.

Our special thanks to those people who played important roles in the creation of this book:

To Gail for her transcriptions—and astute criticism—of the initial class tapes.

To Loretta for her tireless retyping of the many revisions.

To Renni for helping slim the book to a manageable size, and for persuading us to write under our real names.

—CLAUDE AND DOROTHY NOLTE

Contents

Wake Up
in Bed,
Together!

1

Where Are You?

This is a book about how to live with someone for whom you care, about a process called marriage. We recognize, of course, that not all couples who explore this book will be formally married to each other. No matter; our message applies equally to those who have a stable ongoing relationship which, to us, implies a personal commitment to one another's growth.

We are real people, happily married, with grown children, and have functioned as a teaching couple in family-life education and psychology for some twenty years. We believe that a book on sex in marriage should reflect the views and experiences of a happily mated pair rather than those of half a pair or no pair at all! It is our hope that sharing with you how a sexually mature husband and wife think, feel, and conduct their lives may provide insight into your own marriage. In our experience, sexuality and spirituality are not as far apart as most of us were taught, and marriage, when appreciated in this light, is the ideal setting for growth toward self-understanding.

Human beings spend twelve to twenty years obtaining an education to fit them for life and earning a living. Education for sexual harmony and fulfillment is nonexistent, left to chance, the back alley, or a sex manual. This last, admittedly a step forward from "when the time comes you'll know what to do," too often leaves the reader with the feeling that he or she doesn't measure up.

Our work—we call it Sexual Repatterning—has been with couples who were looking for the "more" they sensed was inherent in their relationship. Many had read "all" the books, done all the "right" things. In fact, they were so busy doing all the right things they weren't really enjoying each other.

Having accurate knowledge about sex is important, of course; however, you may not be transmitting what you know about sex, in your head, to your genitals. The Sexual Repatterning we suggest deals specifically with the transition from "I want to, but I can't" to "I want to, and I'm willing to try."

It is not enough just to learn new techniques. The permission and freedom to explore must come from inside.

Sexual Repatterning initially helps you to change the attitudes that keep you from doing this by encouraging you to reevaluate your childhood concepts toward sexuality, to develop the ability to communicate, to say what you feel when you feel it. Sharing with your partner in this way can bring about a new depth in your relationship.

Sexual expression, in our opinion, is a *growth process between two persons.* It includes the ability to sense each other's needs and to fulfill them in ways pleasurable to both. This takes time. There may be barriers to overcome. Do so together, mutually supporting and helping each other.

The goal of Sexual Repatterning is for each couple to achieve a shared physical, mental, and emotional approach to sex and marriage. This means examining your sex life with a fresh outlook, establishing good communication, and developing your love skills.

It *is* important that you take your time and find your own pace. Sexual Repatterning cannot be done overnight. Nor can it be done simply by reading a book—this book or any other. The repatterning is the consequence of the changes that emerge when, after you have read each chapter together, out loud (and preferably in the nude), you *use* this book together.

Most married couples have read sex books but generally not out loud and *not* together. Instead, one person reads a book and tells the other the "interesting" parts, or the part he or she thinks the other should know. We believe that what is important is being aware, as you read, of your responses and reactions: how you feel together, the ideas that run through your minds as you talk them over. Setting time aside to do this on a reasonably regular schedule may be a challenge, especially if there are small children. But people do manage to join bowling leagues, go to the movies, and take up belly-dancing. You can create time together if you choose.

As a starter, make your own appraisal of your love life by responding to the questions that follow. Not all of them are sexual in nature, yet all of them have a bearing on the quality of your sexual relationship. There is no need to "score" yourselves; this is not a test. Simply answer each question honestly.

Both Together

When was the last time you read a book together?

When was the last time you took a walk together?

When was the last time you went swimming nude (or took a bath) together?

When was the last time you sat together, nude, and talked?

When was the last time you tried a new position for sex?

When was the last time you tried something new in bed?

When was the last time you talked, together, about how "it" used to be?

When was the last time you lay quietly, with penetration, and dropped off to sleep that way without an orgasm?

When was the last time you could really "see" the other's point of view, even though you didn't agree with it?

When was the last time you shared an inner feeling with the other?

When was the last time you really looked into each other's eyes?

When was the last time you both had the same idea at the same time?

When was the last time you just held each other, that's all?

When was the last time you said, "Here, let me help you with that?"

For the Man

When was the last time you massaged her, with no sex price tag?

When was the last time you took her to a motel or a resort for the weekend—just the two of you?

When was the last time you held her and let her cry without questioning or "shushing"?

When was the last time you concentrated on bringing her to orgasm but *decided* to skip it for yourself and just enjoy her experience?

When was the last time you confined your lovemaking to above her waist?

When was the last time you kissed her on the mouth, when you *weren't* making love?

For the Woman

When was the last time you felt close to him even though he wasn't there?

When was the last time you thought about his genitals?

When was the last time you unzipped him and fondled his penis, when you weren't in the bedroom?

When was the last time you cheerfully *encouraged* him to have a really great orgasm when you weren't in the mood?

When was the last time you suggested making love in the afternoon?

When was the last time you left your panties off to give him a freer "feel"?

Bedroom experiments will help you in the repatterning process. We don't guarantee that you will find every one of them "sensuous," but when done in the spirit intended they can provide a healthy way to learn about each other, together.

Some of the experiments may be familiar to you. That's OK. Do them anyway, and look for differences, for newness. For one couple an experiment may be "awful," while others may find it fun. Experience and enjoy any or all of the experiments as often as you like. If you feel that having done them once you are satisfied and are finished with them, that's OK too.

We will discuss virtually every human sexual activity. There will be explicit discussion as well as the "how to" of mouth-to-mouth kissing, oral-genital contacts, digital-genital contacts, anal-genital contacts—in fact, the joining of just about each and every protuberance and orifice with which the human species is blessed!

Writing this book has been one of the most challenging experiences we have shared. It required us to go through a repatterning process too. Both of us have had to look at ourselves in a totally new way, question our beliefs, put into words what we feel and think. We are opening ourselves to you and trust that we will be treated with understanding.

Our objective is to help you find fulfillment, "nourishment," comfort, and inspiration; and at least sometimes the special, sacramental quality which characterizes what we call *sexual communion.*

2

Talking and Exploring: Sexual Communication

Mature sexuality, in our concept, is much more than the joining of genital to genital. It is a blending of mental, emotional, and spiritual energies as well, a vital interaction of one whole person with another. It includes a deep communication with a loved one, with one's own body and body parts, with one's innermost feelings.

Simple things like using your sense organs—eyes, ears, nose, hands, mouth—to explore how your partner feels, tastes, and smells are important, as are looking openly at each other, listening to the love sounds you make together, talking freely. You may already be doing most of these things, but are you really aware that you do? Expand your awareness, open yourself to what your senses tell you.

Using your senses does not *have* to be sensual. Let's face it: no one is sexy twenty-four hours a day. Yet the senses are working continuously, giving impressions even during sleep. As you read this, become aware of the position of your legs, the feeling of the air around you; sense the rhythm of your breathing, the sounds in the room. Notice how you first expand your awareness, then contract it as you refocus your attention once more on reading. Do this several times. Be *aware* of yourself and your environment.

Recognize that you send vast amounts of information to others through your body actions. The sigh, the set of the jaw, the gesture, the angle of the eyebrow—all convey messages. What you say with your body is often more revealing than what you say with words. When "all" of you is saying the same thing, it's easier for the other person to "make sense" out of you, and vice versa. When you say one thing and your body says another, the other person senses this too. When all of you agrees to an action, you participate more fully. Lovemaking is bodies "talking together" and reflects what you think and feel.

In a culture that traditionally has asked us to put off our sexuality, to wait, the misconception that "sexual equals genital" is prevalent. Sexuality has been fenced off: "Keep out! Don't pay any attention to it until it's legal." Then, with the magic words of the marriage ceremony, all prohibitions and inhibitions were supposed to disappear.

Sexual ecstasy was to be born full grown as was Venus from the wave! Though this is patently absurd, it has been the easiest way for the majority of parents to deal with their children's awakening sexuality.

Part of Sexual Repatterning is removing these fences. We will be sharing with you our intimate experiences to illustrate how, together, we took down our own fences. We won't ask you to try anything we haven't explored.

Experimentation and exploration are the natural and healthy ways to learn to please each other. Really, all *mutually agreeable* sexual activities are right, good, OK. Only attitudes and beliefs can make mutually desired sexual expressions "bad" or "wrong." Sexual Repatterning asks that you examine your beliefs, that you be aware of those that may be keeping you from becoming mature adults free to explore together new ways of loving. Consider what you yourselves think and feel about the pattern we suggest rather than accepting our beliefs and views without question.

All of this, of course, is not possible unless both partners are able to talk to each other with ease and freedom about sexuality in all its phases. This abil ty, so important to a sexually mature relationship, can be learned. The following should prove useful in helping you handle sexual conversation.

Discussion Sequence

1. *Listen* to What Your Partner Is Saying. Be Sure You Are *Hearing* What Is Being Said.

If you are busily formulating a rebuttal, you will *not* be listening. Set aside what *you* feel or think, be quiet inside, and listen. Your turn will come. Right now your purpose is to get the message. Test *your* understanding. Try asking, "Are you saying———?" or, "I think I understand you. Say it another way so I can be sure." Then try saying it in your words to see if you have it.

2. Find Something Specific That You Can Now *Agree* With in What the Other Said. Voice Your Agreement.

Most intimate discussions get out of hand when both parties focus on what they don't agree on rather than on what they *do*. You can deal more readily with differing views when you first establish a basis for agreement. "Right, I'm glad you said that," or "I feel that way too." When things get touchy, "I do agree with the part you said about ———." When things get sticky, "I agree, that's one way to look at it."

3. Make Your Own Honest Statement of What You Feel or Think about the Situation. Be Brief. You Will Get Another Turn.

The use of "and" can be a way of stringing out your sentence, a monopoly that limits the other person's fair turn. Avoid "but"; your second statement then constitutes a rejection of the position you took in the first place.

• 23

Choose the view that best represents your position and end it with a period, not a "but." Avoid justifying your position with "because." Avoid "always" and "never," and the frequent use of "why" questions. Be specific; say what, where, when.

4. Take Turns Listening and Talking.

In your discussions, *assume* that you may not know all the facts; be flexible. Your goal in talking together—whether or not you're "talking sex"—is to recognize that there are other views and to come to a new view together. Simple everyday communications should be acknowledged and answered, each person giving as much understanding and agreement to the other as possible.

Example

Woman: "How about a movie tonight?" Man: "What's playing?"

There's another, better way of responding. The man might say, "Good idea. Have you checked to see what's playing?" or, "I'm really tired. How about a rain check?" Why are these responses better? Because they avoid answering a communication by simply asking a question—which usually introduces a *new* view and leaves the original communication hanging in the air. It's best to complete the full circle of the message.

There can be times when you may not want to share a particular thought or feeling, or you may not be ready *at that time.* When this happens, say so. Let your partner in on what's happening. In effect, communicate about not communicating. When you feel ready to go back to the thought or feeling, do so.

These guidelines for healthy communication are different from the usual conversational patterns. Practice may be needed before you can use them smoothly. One good way to sharpen up is to listen to conversations in which you are not emotionally involved and in your mind's eye reconstruct them toward the optimum pattern.

Using these guidelines, you may now find it possible to discuss with each other the views and influences that shaped your attitudes toward sexuality. In both overt and covert ways, our sexual patterning reflects the limitations and hang-ups of our parents and others close to us. Begin by talking about your early childhood experiences and experiments. Most of us have such episodes locked away in our memories. For example, did you ever "play doctor"? Did you touch the genital areas? Did you play at intercourse? How did you feel the first time you masturbated?

All sorts of odd notions are formed in childhood, and even though they may be "forgotten," they can nonetheless exert an influence on adult thinking. A person in one of our Sexual Repatterning classes had the idea, as a child, that whenever grown-ups danced they were having sexual intercourse. Another remembered thinking that if two people kissed they were starting a baby. Another had assumed that the baby would be born immediately after intercourse. One man recalled having had no idea that a woman had a vagina. He had assumed that intercourse involved the anus and that the baby was born through the belly button. Another young man remembered asking his girl cousin to remove her panties so he could look. He had started with the buttocks area when her little sister interrupted them, and he never got a look at the front. After he talked about this in class he wondered how he would have reacted if he'd seen she didn't have a penis.

What was the first "dirty" joke you remember hearing? See if you can recall how you felt.

A couple's experiences may be similar or quite different; the important thing is to share together what you find. If you cannot recall any experiences, describe what you heard about the experiments of others, and share with your partner what you imagine *you* might have done. Describe how you feel, right now, as you recall the episode —whether that feeling be embarrassment, excitement, anxiety, guilt, self-consciousness, fear, or amusement. Whatever it is, just state how you feel and stop there. If you are the listener, acknowledge the other's feeling. "See" the situation from his or her point of view.

Keep in mind that you are not playing "confessional"; judgments and forgiveness have no place here. The episode, real or imagined, is over. You are not changing what happened; you are looking together for any effects that such experiences might have on your present attitudes. Discussions like this can help clear away hang-ups you didn't know you had.

One young man shared with some trepidation the memory that as a child he had enjoyed hiding under the back stairs so he could look up women's legs. His wife responded with, "I'm glad you told me that. I used to be self-conscious because I couldn't keep my eyes off the bulge in a man's pants!" They ended up laughing together, reevaluating their childhood concerns.

One young woman spoke of a childhood incident with a neighbor, which she had never mentioned to anyone because it was "terrible." As she began to recall and describe the incident, she realized that the neighbor had, as she put it, "only rubbed on me a bit." The episode, from the adult view, wasn't so "terrible" after all. She decided that the man, not she, should feel the guilt—if anyone should. Granted, some childhood experiences are rather more traumatic than just a little rubbing or touching. But here as well, sharing childhood feelings at the adult level can release hidden emotional distress.

Share the ways your mother and father exchanged affection. Did you see them kissing or holding each other? Did you ever come into the bedroom and find them in bed "doing something"? These are the kinds of experiences to dredge up and talk about together. Can you remember times when what your parents "said" about love or affection did not match what *you* felt from them? Do you feel your parents were relaxed about sexuality or were they tense or anxious or did they pretend it didn't exist? Who was the more open of your parents? With whom did you feel you could talk more freely?

If either partner begins to get uptight in such a discussion, back away for a while. This is not a self-analysis

session; it is an opportunity to reevaluate sexually significant childhood experiences in an essentially pleasant (if
sometimes a bit embarrassing) manner. Take all the time
necessary for these explorations. More ideas may surface
once you begin to feel comfortable with the technique.
After you've become adept at it, you will find that you feel
freer in many ways.

You can establish sensory communication during the
same period in which you are establishing verbal
communication. The experiments that follow are designed
to help you expand your senses, and if you are to benefit
fully from them, please heed this request: use no night-
gowns or pajamas during the process of Sexual Repatterning.

We have received all sorts of complaints on this one: "I
don't like the feel of sheets," or "I get cold," "What if I
have to get up in the middle of the night?" You can put
more blankets on the bed; a robe can be available. The
opportunity for skin-to-skin contact while you are sleeping together is valuable. If you have objections to sleeping
nude, talk about them together. One woman's objection
was quite simple: "I would be too available for sex." We
asked her to say that again and leave out the *too*. She
discovered that being *available* for sex was OK, it was the
too that bothered her. She decided to give it a try and find
out how she felt about it.

A word about the fourth experiment below. You will
be asked really to look at each other when you're both
nude. Some of you may not think that's such a great idea.

We understand. We're not Hollywood types either. We can appreciate how easy it would be for a reader to assume this looking business is fine for young, "sexy" lovers, but for ordinary people—*bleaah!* Just take it from us, we're very ordinary people. What we're talking about *is* for ordinary people. So when the time comes for that experiment, avoid any tendency to apologize for the way you feel about your body or the way you think it looks.

EXPERIMENTS

1. Seeing with Your Hands

Sit nude facing each other, eyes closed. *Do not talk.*

Take turns gently and *slowly* tracing the outline of your partner's face, head, and neck. Allow two minutes. Include ears, nose, mouth, eyes, brow. Notice textures and temperature.

Place one hand on each side of partner's head; be aware of *your* breathing rhythm.

Open your eyes, and share your impressions.

2. Basic Awareness

Repeat this experiment over a period of time until it comes as naturally as breathing.

Close your eyes.

Be aware of the position of your whole body—arms, legs, head, hands, feet.

Be aware of any pressure as you sit or lie down.

Be aware of the rhythm of your breathing, then of your partner's breathing.

Be aware of the room, then the air on your skin, then the sounds in the room.

Now notice the parts of your body that are not relaxed, and change your position if needed.

Be aware of the top of your head.

Open your eyes.

Be aware of your partner, of the room, the furniture, the walls, the colors. Be aware that you are noticing these things.

Compare these experiences with those from the first experiment.

3. Bathing Together

In shower or tub, bathe each other all over—underarms, genital and anal areas, breasts, feet.

Share your feelings and reactions *as you go.* For example, do you find that either or both of you has skipped over any part of the body during the experiment? Do you particularly enjoy washing a certain part? Is there any part of your body that you really didn't want your partner to wash? On the other hand, is there a part you wish you partner would wash more?

This is an experiment to be enjoyed. Have fun!

4. Exploring with the Eyes

After bathing, look at each other, nude. If a full-length mirror is available, look at yourself. Have all the lights on in the room.

Each of you is to get into the positions that will enable the other really to *look* at the areas washed in the bathing experiment, including the crotch. Separate the folds.

Hold a mirror so the other can see too, and don't overlook the anus. A flashlight may help.

Be aware of emotions and reactions and attitudes as

each of you looks. Do you have even slightly negative feelings toward any of your mate's body parts? If so, what is the basis for this? Have you noticed these feelings before? Do you tend to avoid touching or looking at these body parts?

Share aloud, with your partner, these reactions—whether you are looking or being looked at. Avoid explanations or excuses; try saying, "Right now I feel shy" —or "Right now I feel excited"—whatever may be occurring. Don't feel that you must change your mind about how you feel; just be aware of what the feeling is.

At the completion of this experiment, lie together, wrapped in each other's arms, but with no sexual contact. Find a comfortable position in which you can remain until you drop off to sleep.

If you should have feelings of disapproval or approval about these instructions, discuss these too. There is no "right" response or reaction. The point is to be aware of what you feel and to share that with your partner.

5. Massaging Each Other

Massage your partner with an oil or lotion—all over the body, including the nooks and corners. Alternate between slow and fast movements, light and firm pressure.

Tell the massager what feels the best. Each of you may prefer different movements; different responses are fine.

Be aware that sensual can be sexual, but *does not have to be.*

Share your reactions to the massage, your likes and dislikes.

If you encounter sexual stimulation in areas you hadn't considered "stimulating" before, talk about this together. One woman was surprised when her husband used soft movements in her armpits. As she put it, "I got sexy under my arms." There are many areas of the body, other than specifically genital ones, that are capable of sexual and sensual stimulation. Discovering the uniqueness of your own and your mate's bodily responses can be fun. Notice that all orifices, being rich in nerves, can be highly responsive.

After you have finished the mutual massaging, lie close together, with *no* sexual contact. This time, keep your attention on the feeling of your own and your partner's skin, head to toe, as you drop off to sleep.

From time to time we may advocate (or discourage) ideas or activities that may seem to settle a sexual dispute because they coincide with beliefs and/or wishes of one partner. We urge that the "winning mate" avoid any "I told you so" attitude. You are starting on a brand-new adventure together. Don't louse it up by dragging in an old controversy.

If you have been reading the book by yourself, may we suggest you reread this chapter aloud with your mate and plan to go through the rest of the book in the same way. The results are bound to be better. We also suggest that you proceed through the book in an unhurried manner. Give yourself a week or two to do the experiments up to this point and to think about your reactions to them.

3

The "Sex Organ" You Didn't Know You Had

There is a unique muscle structure in the human body which, when strengthened through exercises and correctly used in sexual intercourse, will intensify sexual arousal, the climax itself, and the overall satisfaction for both partners. This can be, for the woman or the man, like discovering they have a "sex organ" they didn't know existed. The vital role of this miraculous muscle—the pubococcygeous (p.c.g. for short)—in a healthy sex life was recognized by the late Arnold H. Kegel, M.D., professor of gynecology at the University of Southern California School of Medicine.

Don't be surprised if you've never heard of it. When Dr. Kegel's work was mentioned a few years ago in a popular magazine, he was swamped by calls from physicians all over the country who wanted to know what this muscle was that their patients were asking about. The doctors had never heard of it either.

Beginning in the early 1940s, Dr. Kegel conducted his research of the p.c.g. and the related muscle areas for over twenty-five years. Of the more than ten thousand women studied, eighty-five percent had poor development of this muscle area and also showed poor sexual response. Those women with good p.c.g. development had good sexual response.

Patients who became aware of the function of the p.c.g. and developed its tone then became capable of mature sexual responses in virtually all cases. Dr. Kegel considered sexual unresponsiveness to be a *physiological* immaturity and attributed it largely to the woman's not knowing how her body is made and how to use it. The psychological aspects—anxiety, fear, worry—he saw as secondary, predictable side-effects of poor performance.

Assume for a moment that a woman can't open a door because she doesn't know to turn the knob, or what muscles to use, and the muscles are too weak anyway. Add to that the insistence of experts that if she can't open the door, there is something wrong with her mind, and you have the picture. That woman doesn't necessarily have a deep-seated psychological problem, although one could develop as her frustrations mount over her inability to open the door. What she *does* lack are knowledge and practice.

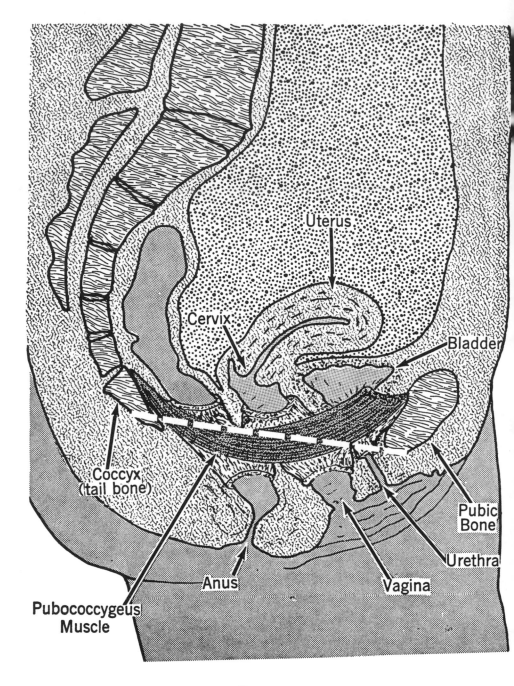

Figure 1

Given these, she could open the door. Given knowledge of the role of the p.c.g. in sexuality, plus practice in using it, the woman can become more responsive.

What, then, *is* the p.c.g.? Visualize it as a hammock or sling, running from the pubic bones in the front of your body to the coccyx at the back (Figure 1). It has three functions: *supportive*, to contain the contents of the abdominal cavity; *sphincteric*, to hold closed the anal, urinary, and, in the woman, the vaginal openings; and *sexual*. If the sling is drooping because the muscle is in poor condition, the perineal area will sag (Figure 2). As a consequence, the various openings will be displaced downward and forward, and the sling will offer little support to the vital organs. A p.c.g. in good tone will be "up"—high and snug. Depending upon whether it's a female or male p.c.g., there will be three openings or two. When the p.c.g. is elastic and firm, it holds these openings closed correctly.

The exercises developed by Dr. Kegel to condition this muscle area enable the woman to contract her p.c.g. at will and to *develop* sexual responsiveness. This ability, used during sexual contact, can create some remarkable sensations for the woman's partner. Men who formerly were quiet during intercourse may begin to moan and exhibit other evidences of intense appreciation when their partners learn to use the p.c.g.

Famous courtesans of history probably had this "p.c.g. skill," as a natural condition or as a result of having developed it—we can only guess. Servicemen returning from the Orient have said that certain prostitutes there exhibited remarkable vaginal muscular skills. They could, for

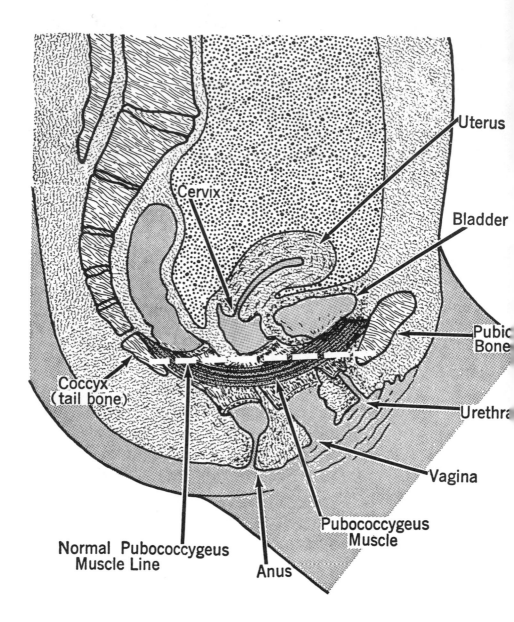

Uterus

Cervix

Bladder

Pubic
Bone

Coccyx
(tail bone)

Urethra

Vagina

Pubococcygeus
Muscle

Normal Pubococcygeus
Muscle Line

Anus

Figure 2

example, take three numbered ping-pong balls into the vagina and manipulate them by using internal muscles! Upon request, they could expel the balls in a specified sequence!

An ex-sailor reported his experience with a young woman on the west coast of Mexico. During her orgasm, he said, "I could feel her vagina milking my penis—it was terrific!" If she had no orgasm, the action didn't occur. When he asked her to do this, just for him, she explained, "It happens when I come. I can't do it myself." He wanted to know how she learned it, but she could only say, "It was like learning to walk. I don't know how."

Further study by Kegel (and others, at the Mayo Clinic) has shown that the nerve endings in the vaginal region are in the body of the p.c.g. muscle, not in the lining of the vagina, where earlier investigators had looked— without finding them. Now we can understand the importance of being able to contract the p.c.g. A firm pressure compresses the vaginal lining, and thereby permits the movement of the penis to stimulate the nerves. It's quite an arrangement, if you think about it. If a woman contracts her p.c.g. a little, the nerves respond a little, which means she contracts it more, which means the nerves get more stimulation, and so on. This sequence leads to the highly rewarding "overall" feeling in the really mature internal sexual response of the woman. Stimulation of the clitoral area alone usually does not activate the nerves in the p.c.g. and therefore does not produce this particular form of sexual response.

For the nerve stimulation to be possible, the p.c.g. must

be in good tone. External pressure applied to the p.c.g. —for example, if the woman "pushes down" with her abdominal muscles—will *not* excite the nerves. Contraction pressure must come from within the p.c.g. itself. In the case of one couple who consulted us, the wife thought she had good p.c.g. control because she could push her husband's penis out when she contracted what she thought was the p.c.g. It turned out that she was using her belly muscles—the wrong thing to do. A p.c.g. contraction grasps the penis but does not expel it.

Another couple wondered if you could get the pressure in the p.c.g. by expanding the vagina, as with a very thick penis. Would this stimulate the nerves? No, that won't work either—unless, the p.c.g. is in good tone and is contracted by the woman.

The nerves are concentrated in spots, or centers, located within the middle third of the length of the vagina. Imagine that you are looking into the vagina of a woman lying on her back with her legs drawn up. Imagine, also, a clock face inside the vagina. The centers would be located, relative to the clock, at about 4:00 and 8:00. Some women have auxiliary spots at 2:00 and 10:00. A woman may be a "lefty" or a "righty" with regard to which side has the greater response.

For many women it is as though these centers have been sleeping. They have never been awakened during the sexual experience. They *can* be awakened; they can function. First they must be located.

The woman lies on her back, knees drawn up. The man quite slowly (taking eight to ten seconds) inserts a well-lubricated finger into the vagina and moves it inward *very gently* along, say, the 4:00 position. The woman is to be aware of what she feels, physically, as he first enters and as his finger progresses, and voice those feelings. The man continues touching gently until the woman senses a difference in the feeling. When such a spot is located, the man often will have the feeling that his finger tip has just found a "dimple" in the wall of the vagina. *Light* stimulation of this center with the finger tip will help awaken the woman to awareness of her internal (vaginal) response-feeling in addition to her more commonly experienced external (clitoral) response. The man should check all four positions; one, two, three, or four centers may be present.

In locating them, the woman watches for any change in sensation. In the course of his clinical work, Dr. Kegel would notice the surprise in a woman's voice when a center was located. She would say, "Oh, yes. I feel the difference!" or, "Yes. That's the spot!" Once a woman has been brought to an awareness of both the existence and the location of the centers, she can *feel* with them. Then the ridge around the glans of the man's penis, slowly stroking, can gently "remind" the woman of her responsive centers. It can, that is, if the man's movements are slow and *if* he can delay his responses long enough to give the woman time for her sensations to build. (How the man learns to slow down will be discussed later in this chapter.)

The position of these sexual centers is not deep inside, usually about two finger joints or less. That's not far, which is important. If a finger doesn't have to reach "way up" to encounter them, neither does a penis. Conse-

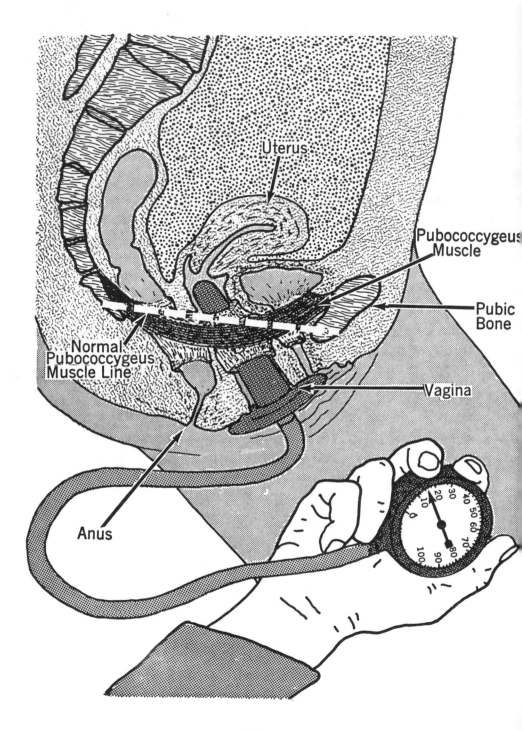

Figure 3

quently, a long penis is not necessarily required to contact the centers. If the woman's p.c.g. is in good tone, the vagina is capable of accommodation to a longer penis (within reason) or to a shorter one. If her vagina can adapt, the size of the penis inside it is unimportant. On the other hand, a woman who has poor p.c.g. tone may not be able to accommodate to penis variations as effectively.

Dr. Kegel developed an instrument, the *perineometer*, to measure the strength of the p.c.g. (Figure 3). The device consists of a rubber bladder that is inserted into the vaginal opening. The woman contracts her p.c.g., and the strength of the muscle is shown as a reading on a dial. The healthy p.c.g. will register from thirty to seventy on the scale. Another good "perineometer" is a husband's penis. If a woman contracts as hard as she can and asks her husband, "How did that feel?" and he replies, "How did *what* feel?"—it's clear she has a way to go on her p.c.g. development! Noting the change in the strength of her grasp on two fingers inserted in the vagina is another way to check the woman's progress.

A quick and easy way to improve the functioning of the p.c.g. is to learn to control urination. Working with the sphincteric function of the p.c.g. will lead to your awareness of its sexual function.

The first of the special exercises is to be done on the toilet. Whether you are male or female, sit on the toilet to urinate. Spread your legs slightly, and don't contract the muscles on the insides of the thighs. Relax and start urinating. Then, shortly after you start, stop. Now, be aware of what you are doing as you stop. After you send the signal to "stop," *listen;* has the urine indeed stopped, or are you still drizzling along? The better the tone of the p.c.g., the easier it is to stop the flow in midstream. If you can't, take heart; this exercise is designed to help you out of the situation. Once again, go back and think *how* you try to stop the flow. You should not be squeezing your buttocks or thighs together; you should not be holding your breath. None of these muscular activities is involved.

Instead, learn to stop the flow of urine with your legs slightly apart and easy, the buttocks and abdominal wall relaxed. Send your awareness inside yourself. Ask yourself, "What do I do to stop urinating?" Practice each time you urinate. Start it, and stop it. When you have a full bladder, take care that you barely start the flow before you shut it off again, otherwise it may be more difficult to stop. And don't ever force the stream to gush out, which tends to weaken the p.c.g. *Allow* it to flow. When you can stop the flow easily, discontinue the toilet exercise.

Now for the next step. The first thing in the morning, before you get out of bed, locate the p.c.g. and contract it once. Say to yourself, "There it is, there." Be *aware,* in your insides, where this muscle is located and how you are contracting it. Just saying the words won't work; truly sensing the location and the movement *will.* Now swing your legs over to the floor. Again, be aware of the p.c.g. Contract a few times, *slowly, not jerkily.* Hold and then release. Do this exercise until you really get a sense of your "insides."

In this second stage of the exercises, become aware of the p.c.g. periodically through the day, and contract the muscle twenty-five times. Increase the number of times you do this in a day until you build up to eight times per day. Stay at that level of frequency for several weeks. Then drop back to doing a few sets of twenty-five contractions every day. Don't forget to establish awareness before contracting; going through the motions without awareness will not yield satisfactory results.

You can strengthen self-awareness when doing this exercise by thinking "contract" and "lift" rather than "squeeze." Imagine that you are standing erect, and then imagine a line running right through your body straight up to the top of your head. As you activate the p.c.g., think of a "lifting" action along this line. In other words, you "contract up" with a feeling of lifting the floor of the pelvis.

For the woman, the lifting action is at the vaginal outlet; for the man, at the base of the penis and scrotum. You will sense an upward squeezing "feeling" when you are doing it correctly. Do not push with the abdominal muscles. Contracting them, as in expelling a bowel movement, will produce the opposite of the lifting action intended. When you practice, place your hand on your abdomen to be sure you are not pushing with the abdominal muscles.

As their ability to use the p.c.g. increases, some women find the exercise stimulating enough to produce a sexual response. That's fine; consider it a bonus for being diligent, for here is an area where diligence pays.

The woman who has developed awareness and control of the p.c.g. can be taught to transfer the sexual sensations of the clitoris to her internal sexual centers. Most women don't known that they can transfer stimuli from the clitoris to the inside, or that they can *feel* in the vagina. But once a woman has experienced even a modest degree of internalization of her sensations, she knows that the clitoris isn't the only center of sexual feeling and sensation.

So far, we've discussed the importance of the p.c.g. for the woman. A well-toned, truly functional p.c.g. is equally useful for the man. He can contract it to produce stimulating "wiggles" of his penis inside the woman to create a pleasant sensation for her. It can assist him in maintaining an erection for a longer period. Prolonged lovemaking, of course, enables the man to enjoy the depth of sensual experience that is missing in the "bam, bam, thank you ma'am" encounter.

The average male experiences scant differentiation between sexual arousal and the ejaculative explosion. All the nuances possible between these extremes are jammed together by his rapid drive toward climax (five minutes following penetration is usual). When he develops p.c.g. awareness and tone, he can control, direct, and slow this response. The different levels of response can then be experienced, be savored. Remember, the heightening of sensations for both partners comes through the *slow* movement of the glans over the sexual centers. This ability to take it easy allows the time for stronger feeling to build in the woman and enables her to internalize and totally experience powerful sexual sensations as the lovemaking progresses.

At this point, you can progress to a fundamental

method for the repatterning of both partners at the same time. Lie nude on your sides, facing each other, and you're ready to begin.

For the Woman

Put your upper leg, with the knee bent, over his upper leg. Now take his penis in your hand, and move the head of the penis over your pubic hair, then the lips of the vulva, at the rate of about ten strokes a minute. If necessary, use two fingers to spread the lips and make the clitoris more accessible.

Now move the penis in a *slow*, stroking manner and rub it around and on the clitoris. Remember, this can produce a strong arousal in the man; check with him often and pause for him to "catch his breath."

As you begin to feel aroused, maintain the slow, stroking movements and visualize in your mind's eye these feelings moving from the clitoral area, between the labia, then approaching the opening of the vagina. Help this internalization of the feelings along by moving the head of the penis from the clitoral area further back each stroke, until the head goes inside a bit. Continue slowly, going in and out, deeper each time. This could take ten to twenty minutes. Continue visualizing the pleasurable sensations as moving inside the vagina. Notice changes in your responses as you begin to feel these sensations as *being inside*.

Now release your hold on the penis as he takes over the movements.

For the Man

With your penis inside, move *slowly* about ten strokes per minute. This rate will be much slower than your normal patterning, but it's important in lengthening staying power. With slow, rhythmic movements, you can avoid pushing yourself over the brink. If you begin to feel the start of the rapid rise of sensation to orgasm, you can slow further or stop in time to let the feeling subside. If you're breathing rapidly, the chances are you're stroking too fast; the rate of breathing should be about the same as the stroking. If you must stop to avoid too much sensation, begin very slowly when you start again.

We suggest that you keep your eyes open. Closing them can start a change in the sympathetic nervous system that signals the ejaculation; opening them tends to suppress this action. You may find you're closing your eyes without realizing, so watch it!

For the woman, closing the eyes is OK. In fact, if she has her eyes open, and senses the onset of strong feelings, closing them can enhance her response.

This exercise is crucial to the process of Sexual Repatterning. For the woman, it is the way she learns to internalize her sexual sensations. The man learns to slow his response. Use this exercise as a prelude to your lovemaking until you are both proficient.

For men who continue to have difficulty holding off ejaculation: try, for a while, using one or even two condoms, in addition to the slow movements—even if condoms are not your method of birth control. This will limit the stimulation received by the penis and allow you to learn to experience heightened sensations without rapid ejaculation. As control is developed, drop to one condom and then eliminate them entirely.

From the lore of the prostitute, we've borrowed some help for the man who really has a hair-trigger. This method calls for the woman to masturbate him with her hand until he feels the beginning of the rapid rise. When he tells her, she encircles the head of his penis just under the glans with two fingers, and with her thumb on the underside, and squeezes firmly. This pressure reduces the feeling of an impending orgasm. It's a little like holding your finger under your nose when you have to sneeze. The man's erection may subside with this squeeze, and that's OK: continue alternately the stimulation and the pressure, perhaps five or six times. In three to six weeks, usually less, the man's patterning will be retrained.

Whatever repatterning method he uses, the man must focus on identifying the first flicker of the rapid rise in sensation and slow down or perhaps stop during inter-course—long enough to allow the sensations to subside. Resist the strong temptation to keep on stroking at the same pace. You may feel that it's too late anyway or that you can go a few more strokes and then slow down. Don't fall for these traps. If you must stop, do so in midstroke if need be. Trying to reduce the stimulation by withdrawing can be disastrous: the vagina stimulates the penis the most during the out movement, so that is the wrong way to go! The best solution is to learn to recognize that initial upsurge as soon as it starts and slow down right then. Your body won't want to, of course, and it takes practice, but the rewards are worth the effort.

During sexual contacts of longer duration, lubrication can be important. If a woman's supply is scanty, saliva is a convenient supplement. (Curiously enough, we find Claude's saliva works better than Dorothy's; we don't know why.) At times, if saliva isn't sufficient, you may want to use one of the various commercial lubricants such as K.Y. Jelly. The water-base types are better for *frequent* usage; they tend to match a woman's natural secretions and are more compatible with her membranes.

For those of you who are reading this book aloud together as we have recommended, congratulations! For those of you who are not, again we suggest that you give it a try. You could have a great deal of fun, improve your love skills, gain in self-awareness and intensity of response, and get to know you partner better. True, you might wind up acknowledging that you're not yet the lovers you could be, which you probably suspected in the first place. Together, you might decide what you'd like to do about that.

EXPERIMENTS

1. How Does It Feel to You?

Discuss this chapter with each other. Express your moods, your reactions, your agreements, your disagreements with what we have said. Avoid intellecutal responses; see if you can "sense" our message. Keep your communications short. Respect the other person's point of view.

2. How Long Can You Last?

Talk frankly about the staying power of the man—at this point, thirty seconds is no better or no worse than ten minutes. Whatever his staying power has been in the past, it can be different in the future, provided he goes along with the instructions.

3. Finding the "Sex Organ" You Didn't Know You Had

Locate and gently stimulate the sexual centers as described on pages 40–41.

4. Basic Sexual Repatterning

Do the exercise on pages 47–50.

5. The Penis Meets the Sexual Centers

Choose a position that is comfortable for both.

Do the clitoral/vaginal stroking with penis (Experiment 4).

Slowly insert the penis.

Using ten strokes per minute, make diagonal movements. "Aim" for sexual centers; enter *only enough* to touch them.

The woman tells the man which direction and depth feel best and seem to enhance her internal sensations. Change position if necessary.

If there is too much stimulation for the man, he should slow down and be sure eyes are open. Usually, if he allows the strong sensations to subside several times, his brain "gets the message" and stops turning on the ejaculation signals. Then he can go on without the need to slow or stop as often. While that may not happen the first time, it will sooner or later.

What if the explosion button does get pushed and he "blows it?" That's normal, it can happen. Practice can change how *often* it happens. If he keeps working toward this goal of slow, side-to-side rhythmic movement, he'll acquire the skill. Later, when his p.c.g. is developed, he can contract it as a means of avoiding ejaculation.

4

Orgasm: Why? When? What Kind?

"Get it up, get it in, get it, get it out!" Orgasm, orgasm, who's got the orgasm?! Is it clitoral or vaginal? Big or little? "Multiple" or not? All too often, we have found that orgasm is *the* sexual issue for American couples.

Is the female orgasm clitoral or vaginal? We feel that if more reporting were done by sexually mature couples, this particular controversy would disappear. But happy couples whose sexual relationship is mutually fulfilling do not, of course, seek help, and so their experience does not come to the attention of researchers.

Here's the way we see the matter. On the surface, it

may seem that there is no such thing as a vaginal orgasm simply because, in the case of most women, the p.c.g. is in poor tone and she is unable to transfer her sensations from the clitoris to her higher sexual centers. The woman who is unable to transfer, to internalize, stays strictly at the clitoral response level.

Dorothy describes her experience before she consulted Dr. Kegel: "For practical purposes my orgasms, if and when, were clitoral, requiring finger stimulation by my partner. I had my first vaginally centered orgasm with Claude. Dr. Kegel's patient instruction helped me to become aware of sexual expression as a natural, normal physiological function. Also, my exercise patterning established this *awareness* of function. Finally, Claude's gentleness, slowness, and complete command of his own response were tremendously important. I won't forget that 'first' experience.

"Looking back, I see a gradual growth toward what Claude and I call 'total response.' Now I experience levels of orgasm which build toward this. For me, there are clitoral orgasms *and* vaginal orgasms *and* clitoral/vaginal orgasms—a whole spectrum from one to the other, including both at the same time. My clitoral response feels more focused, frenetic, and locally intense. With the vaginal response the rise is slower and more expansive—and with the climax itself I feel a greater depth of feeling, or fulfillment, that is emotional as well as physical. Each experience is different in its own special way."

As each woman learns to recognize her levels of response and feeling in her vagina, we believe that she too can find her own high points. She can allow these to build and will be able to identify her "mini-orgasms," which gradually develop into her total responsiveness. The main point here is to appreciate each sexual experience for itself, not to strive for the ultimate "maxi-orgasm," which tends to limit enjoyment by establishing only one type of experience as pleasurable.

When a man has made love with a woman who has awareness of her p.c.g. and its function and can experience total response, he knows the difference between the mini- and the maxi-orgasms his partner experiences and derives a variety of pleasures according to her mood of sexual experiencing.

The fact that a controversy over clitoral *versus* vaginal orgasms exists is understandable in light of the fact that most women and many doctors are unaware of the p.c.g. muscle and its significance. For the woman who develops her p.c.g. muscle and achieves internalization of her sexual response, the controversy is meaningless.

It's interesting to note that orgasm can occur in the woman who has no clitoris! A missionary and his wife, both trained in Dr. Kegel's methods, took their knowledge with them to Africa. In that particular region, until a few years ago, a clitorectomy was performed routinely when a girl reached the age of seven or eight—to insure that when she grew to maturity, sex would be uninteresting and she would have no inclination to stray from her husband's bed.

With the passing of this custom and exposure to Western ideas, some young African married women wanted a more complete sexual experience. Many who did the p.c.g. exercises regularly began to have *vaginal* orgasmic responses!

In our culture, the man is held accountable for his wife's orgasm. This notion seriously undermines the *sharing* of pleasure and responsibility for pleasure that characterizes mutually satisfying sex. The wife should have the opportunity, and the necessary time, for her self-expression: to generate her own internal awareness, develop her willingness and ability to respond to her own sexuality. Yet the poor guy is not only supposed to get her hot, he's supposed to make her come, with strong emphasis on *make*. The latest fad demands he make her come many times. Psychologically, emotionally, we think this is a bad scene.

But who said you have to have an orgasm in the first place? We are presenting a quite different view. We believe that the *experiencing* and *sharing* and the *responding* are of primary importance. Dorothy says, "If I take care of my feelings, my own sensations, enjoy them and allow them to build, the satisfaction takes care of itself. It's important, of course, that Claude as a sexually mature male can provide the time for my responses to develop.

"Our sexual contacts are *one* form of meaningful communication between us. The emphasis is not on who comes or who doesn't. Against a basic background of feeling good about each other and a sense of fulfillment in our physical sharing, the 'have to' is not emphasized— whatever form our sexual contacts may take. This makes possible several combinations: we both come or I do and

Claude doesn't or Claude does and I don't or neither of us does."

It's hard for most couples to realize that this last "combination"—neither partner experiencing orgasm—can be enjoyable in its own way, is in *no* way the disaster we've been taught to see it as.

"On occasion," Dorothy says, "I like to enjoy experiencing my husband's responses while we're making love. Sometimes I'm not interested in having an orgasm. I may just want an internal massage—Claude's penis feels good moving inside me. I feel relaxed, I experience myself in a different way. A woman can like feeling her vagina is filled, an awareness of the firmness of the penis, something she can hold onto that lets her feel her softness and her husband's hardness at the same time. For me, this is a uniquely feminine response that's difficult to put into words."

"That works both ways," says Claude. "At times, for me, it's great to feel my wife responding, to experience *her* responses. What's important is the awareness of our being together."

Now and then it can be good to climax simultaneously. But even an experienced couple doesn't have *that* experience every time, and we don't consider it a goal. It's great when it turns out that way, and yet, in the intensity of your own response, you can miss the delight of experiencing your partner's. Generally, we lean toward the woman climaxing first. If she has p.c.g. awareness and good muscle tone, her natural contractions will bring the man along.

In our experience we have found the absence of an

orgasm to produce no psychological or physiological ill effects in the man or the woman—unless, of course, non-orgasm is the rule rather than the exception.

On the positive side, the ability to remain together for a prolonged period, by choice, leads to warm, shared feelings that further heighten sexual communication. Some of our students have reported a "beautiful glow" continuing for extended periods after they have been together for an hour or more—whether there was orgasm or not. After sex, both partners can be aware of energy, vitality, fulfillment, and deep satisfaction in the closeness.

Something to remember: stay together after the climax of one or both of you to allow the feelings of love, warmth, and affection to permeate. The afterglow, lasting as long as an hour, can be lovely. This is no time to do a "streaking" number to wash up! If we make love in the morning, and communion has been particularly close, we both experience the continuation of this glow for a few hours or throughout the day.

The emphasis on having to have an orgasm brings us to the acceptance by both men and women of the "tyranny of the orgasm." The importance of the orgasm has made it a threat that hangs over their heads. You may remember the riddle: what's the difference between annoyance and catastrophe? The first time a man can't make it the second time, that's annoyance; but the second time he can't make it the first time, that's catastrophe!

Way off target! That man has the opportunity to enjoy waiting and not rushing his partner, if he would look at it that way. The tyranny of the female orgasm adds to the man's frustration, because now he's got to make sure she has an orgasm too. The woman frustrates herself by feeling cheated. If we can do nothing more than help you back away from the idea that your only goal in sexual loving is orgasm or ejaculation, and substitute the attitude of "OK, that happens too, but it's not the sole purpose, nor is it the sole satisfaction," we will have accomplished a great deal.

Occasionally we encounter the curious situation where a woman believes that she fails to have orgasms, when actually she is failing to recognize the experience for what it is. The fact is that female orgasmic response varies in its intensity and character from person to person, from occasion to occasion. Our cultural imagery, as well as pornographic books and movies, give the impression that women experiencing orgasm faint or thrash about as if in a violent seizure or exhibit uncontrollable body responses or are skyrocketed into multiple orgasms every time. This is an unrealistic picture of sexual intercourse, to say the least. Some women may react this way, some of the time. But if you expect sex to be like this, you are opening yourself, whether man or woman, to frustration and disappointment.

A woman who consulted us explained that she was one of those who enjoyed sex but did not have orgasms. Her husband did "all the right things," but she was just not responsive enough. Dorothy asked what she *did* feel, during and after. The woman said she enjoyed pleasant sensations in her vagina, which kept getting stronger and then subsided. Afterward she felt happy and snuggly and sleepy. This woman assumed she had to respond more violently, as her husband did during ejaculation, to consider her response as an orgasm.

Dorothy observed that, from the description, this woman's experiences sounded like mini-orgasms. She recommended that she concentrate her attention on her good feelings—accept them, welcome them, encourage them to build—and avoid focusing on "having an orgasm." Later, the woman confirmed that the mini-orgasms were indeed building to greater intensity.

A woman may be apprehensive about "letting herself go," about allowing the climax to occur and fully experiencing her responses. The woman may have been warned as a girl: "Your sex urge will take you over—you'll lose control," or something similar. The experiments in repatterning will help her to open herself gradually and with confidence.

However, as a result of early bedroom disappointments, or perhaps the aftereffects of arguments, a woman may have developed a reluctance to allowing herself to "open up." Deep down inside she may fear that if she were to do so, she might be "vulnerable" to some vague (or not so vague) harm or manipulation. She may resist permitting her mate to see how deeply he would affect her were she to respond.

Nor is the male immune to feelings of vulnerability when it comes to letting go sexually. He too may be reluctant to let his mate see the depth of response he could have. He may fear that she'd make fun of him: he may be hung up on the notion that it's unmanly to feel deeply.

Perhaps he's afraid of what he would feel or do—or imagines he would—if he did let go.

At this point in your Sexual Repatterning, begin to use your natural sensitivity to each other in a positive way. Feeling too open is just as unhappy a situation as being closed off. Each of you needs to feel OK about letting the other in on your "weak" side—no one can be strong all the time. It is good to be able to experience your softness, male *or* female, to find a balance in your tough and tender feelings. Both these responses can be part of a healthy sex life. Find ways to *sense* the "other side" of yourselves. Play square; avoid taking unfair advantage of the other as you begin to feel more open.

Strange as this may sound, men too may be confused about what an orgasm is for them! The usual idea is: when a man ejaculates, that's an orgasm. Webster's definition of orgasm is: "the climax of the sex act." Ejaculation may complete the sex act, but it does not necessarily mean achieving a climax of the *possible* emotional response.

Most men can recall times when "going off" left them still unsatisfied; they wanted more. That's partly what we're talking about, but not all. The man who has learned to pace himself, to slow his response, can experience an orgasm without ejaculation that may surpass in sensation and fulfillment the "ordinary" ejaculative variety. In our experience, the difference is not unlike that between clitoral and vaginal response.

At best, attempting to describe sexual feelings is difficult. We've compared our impressions and have come to the view that, for us, the character of Claude's total sexual response turns out to be very like Dorothy's!

Discovering this has helped us to understand better and to appreciate each other's experience in sex. We see sexuality as a part of human loving; clitoral response as a *part* of the woman's total responsiveness, not the whole of it.

The woman with a well-developed p.c.g. and awareness of her sexual centers learns not only to feel with her vagina, but to caress and hold with it too. Lovemaking for thirty minutes or more brings to the man and woman a series of ascending peaks of sensation, with small dips in between for the man, rather than the swift rise and fall of the solely ejaculative style. The "coming," after this buildup, tends to last longer and provide a more powerful "rolling" climax. The level of sensation may be so deeply pleasurable that the man may be content without ejaculation—then, if he allows his movements to become slower, he can relax into the "warm glow" of his partner's response.

As with other activities in this universe, the sex life of a happy, well-mated couple can assume a cyclic up-and-down pattern, a rhythm, provided it is *permitted* to do so. Most couples are unprepared for the first time sexual interest or activity subsides—a frightening but perfectly natural occurrence. In their disappointment they may accept the usual cynical attitudes toward love and marriage and give in to defeat before the game has started. If they only *knew* about this simple rhythm in their sexuality, they could greet its appearance with understanding and recognize it as normal, to be appreciated as a forerunner of even better things to come.

In our experience these periods of quietude have represented a form of sexual hibernation. When we have resumed a more active sexual relationship, the intensity, the diversity, and the downright degree of satisfaction have been markedly enhanced. At *our* first downward dip we were silently saying wistful goodbyes to the deeply rewarding experiences we had shared. Fortunately we talked about our feelings, even if somewhat hesitantly. Finding that we had a common concern eased the stress and the anxiety. Through this sharing we became aware that the subsidence was actually the opportunity for our sexual expression to gather momentum for the next upswing. Thus it has gone, wave after wave, with each peak higher than the last.

Couples with whom we work have reported similar experiences. Having learned about the subsidence, they accept its appearance without disappointment, as the natural rhythm of a growing relationship. This can be a time to strengthen other facets of marriage, to improve communication and the sharing of inner feelings. It can be a time to meet the sexual needs and desires of one's mate in different ways. It provides an opportunity to build trust factors into the overall relationship. As you continue to express warmth and affection toward each other, this, in itself, creates a nourishing atmosphere for new levels of relating to emerge.

The rhythm of sexual desire, with its high points and low, can offer lovers a serious adjustment challenge. This is the time to be wary of alluring traps. It's the time of the straying eye: would somebody else be better? This "easy out" is all too frequently chosen by one mate or the other.

From our experience we have heard clear messages. It's good to be in touch with one's own love rhythm and to tune in on what each feels inside toward the other. This becomes a mature reaching together for the next step, while trusting one's senses. Consider how subtle, and demanding, is this form of courting. The original courtship was sparked by longing for the unknown, the mysterious. The renewed courtship calls for skillful wooing, with more originality, more sensitivity to the wishes and desires of the mate, whom one now knows, with whom there is less mystery. Young couples who discuss, together, their own love rhythm begin early in their relationship to work *with* nature. They will require fewer adjustments in their later years.

EXPERIMENTS

1. What Are Your Orgasms Like?

Talk together about your orgasmic experiences. Share the kinds of feelings and sensations you have and what you would *like* to experience.

Avoid "shoulds." Think and express "coulds," which allow more freedom of choice. Avoid beginning a sentence with "if only." Say what you *want*.

2. Can You "Let Go"?

Discuss what "letting go" sexually means to you and what your attitudes are. Would it be "safe"? Would it be some "wild" thing? Use your imagination.

3. Kiss/Lick from Head to Toe

The receiver is given a shower or bath.

Then kiss/lick the receiver from head to toe, thoroughly, everywhere.

Receiver focuses on feelings and sensations. They can become strong—that's OK!

Share reactions (pleasant/unpleasant).

Repeat the experiment with the other person as receiver.

Lie close together without penetration until you fall asleep.

While kissing and licking, you may be having an internal debate with yourself that runs something like this:

A: "I'm getting near the anal area!"

B: "You know what the instructions were, get into all the nooks and corners!"

A: "Yes, but it might be dirty!"

B: "The book said to give a shower first. You did a good job, didn't you?"

A: "It seems like it could be nasty even if it's clean."

B: "Where'd you get an idea like that?"

A: "Well, everybody knows . . . oh, I don't know."

B: "Sounds to me like you're just hung up in some old ideas. How about taking a chance?"

If a man or woman considers an area barely an inch away from the testicles or the vagina to be "nasty," this feeling can inhibit sexual freedom. The purpose of this experiment is to help you feel good about all your body parts and body functions. When you establish and maintain an attitude that a part of your body is dirty or bad, and therefore unacceptable, you reject it, withdraw from it, alienate it from the "good" parts of your body. One can't withdraw and enjoy simultaneously.

In sharing your feelings and thoughts, remember, no judgments! It isn't that you're right and the other person is wrong. We don't expect the other person to talk you out of your point of view or vice versa. Sometimes, with discussions, you might, *within yourself,* assume that another point of view is better than your original one. Bear in mind, a point of view is just that, a position from which to *observe* something.

4. No Two Ways about It

This week, notice the times when you feel "two ways" sexually about yourself or your partner. Are these familiar or unfamiliar feelings? Notice how you express them with your body. Be aware of any tensions—and of your responses to them.

5

Sexual Abundance

As you may have noticed by now, this book does not use the term *foreplay*, let alone devote a chapter to it. Emphasis on foreplay, we think, has been overdone. Sure, affection and love stimulation *are* appropriate. The trouble is that such a fetish has been built around using the proper methods to get the woman "hot" that yet another layer of boredom has been placed on lovemaking. There is no genuine excitement and anticipation—it's all so routine. The woman may be thinking, "First he'll kiss my mouth, then he'll rub my nipples, then he'll. . .."; while the man thinks, "Is she ready yet? I wonder if this is enough."

As we see it, the prelude is *intended* to imply affection, loving tenderness, a deep desire to please one's mate. These are attitudes that belong in a couple's lives each day, not just when one partner or the other wants sex. The emphasis on "doing all the right things to get her ready," if not matched in daily living with considerate affection, is more likely to wind up as a turn-off rather than a turn-on. Clitoral stimulation, breast fondling, and so on can give the impression that the man is bartering these gestures in exchange for a piece of tail, doing them because he's supposed to rather than because he wants to and enjoys it. As one woman expressed her feelings, "Don't do me any favors!"

Overemphasizing the prelude tends to de-emphasize the importance of day-to-day thoughtfulness and affectionate gestures, by women and men alike. Through the years we've exchanged expressions of affection as a daily, ongoing pattern: a kiss on the cheek, the back of the neck, the earlobe; a short hug, face-to-face or just quietly enfolding each other; strokes or pats. Cuddling or snuggling in bed, cupping a breast, stroking pubic hair or penis —these are happening whether sex is in sight or not. We both find the other "feels good" to touch anywhere, any time.

As you proceed with your Sexual Repatterning, we hope you are becoming aware that sexuality is even more than a head-to-toe experience: it is ongoing in *time* as well. It is the sharing of loving, warm feelings out of the bedroom as well as in. So while we do discuss things you can do during the prelude, we prefer to allow your own spontaneity to govern what, when, and how long. Spontaneity may call for a long prelude or a short one. In any case, it should be mutual rather than one-sided.

Another vital ingredient for rewarding and satisfying sexuality is variety—as to when, where, and in what position. Explore as many different times, locations, and positions as you can, then use the ones that suit you best.

Most marriage manuals describe numerous positions. The trouble is, the instructions may be difficult to remember, even if you can figure them out from the description. If you are experimenting with the book in one hand, by the time you've finished explaining—"Well, honey, you put your heel up here and your elbow there, and you wind your other leg around this way"—both of you could be cooled off. Looking at a picture is a better approach; one good look can suffice.

A paperback called *Intercourse* is worth purchasing by mail order if your bookstore can't get it. It contains pictures of a husband and wife, in the nude, demonstrating a number of positions. Another book, *A Happier Sex Life*, contains photos of wooden mannequins to illustrate many postures. The two-volume *Sex in Marriage* includes excellent color photographs of numerous positions. If nothing else, this book provides another way to cast aside sexual shackles just by *looking* together.

The motion pictures that have been made ostensibly to demonstrate sexual positions do show variety, but the technique is poor, with movements that are fast, even frantic. If such a movie comes your way, go see it by all means if you like, but stay with your *slow movements* until your repatterning is well established.

Positions that require the full weight of one partner upon the other are not the best for continuous use during a lengthy sexual contact. The man-on-top position, for instance, is the hardest for him to use. He must support his full weight on his knees and his elbows, or he'll squash his wife. When considering a contact for as long as an hour, he's likely to feel, "no way!" As *a* method the man on top works fine, but as the *only* position, no!

As couples work toward longer contact with slow movement, they find the side positions more suitable. As the Roman poet Ovid expressed it, "Of all the ways of love, the best by far is to lie side by side, withall." Varieties of the side-by-side position can be used: face-to-face or face-to-back. A combination called the Von Urban position, in which the woman lies on her back and the man lies on his side, is especially recommended (see Experiment 5). This position allows both partners to be relaxed and still offers maximum opportunity for movement. Also, a couple may drop off to sleep comfortably after climax in this position, without withdrawal.

The location of the sex organs in each woman's body affects her response to a given position. The placement of the cervix can make a difference, as can the clitoral placement, high or low, and whether or not it is hooded. The location of the vaginal opening, whether forward or more to the rear, can monitor her "best" posture. Because of organ placement, some women may find that they particularly enjoy rear entry.

Generally, we think the selection of the desired position should be up to the woman. She should remember, however, that some positions provide a wider range of sensation for the man; his penis can contact the vaginal wall or the cervix differently. This can occur especially with rear-entry methods, where the underside of the glans, the most sensitive part of the penis, contacts the ridgy region on the forward vaginal wall.

Because rear entry is the method animals use in mating, some women may have the feeling it is degrading or abnormal. Actually, rear entry has been and still is a favorite in other cultures, in the Middle East, the Orient, and elsewhere. We like to use this method now and then; the kneeling variety is particularly pleasurable for us. The man can use both hands to move his wife's hips toward and away from him. The motion will be gratifying to both.

During lovemaking, the movements made by the woman are just as meaningful as those of the man. Once she knows about them, she has a variety at her command. She must be willing to explore and exercise a little to become proficient. There can be small circular movements or a shaking-type movement with the pelvis. There's the whole spectrum of what she can do with her p.c.g., once she has developed it. A rich variety of sensations for both results when she simply "turns her tail under." This is a special pelvic movement similar to a stripper's "bump" but done *slowly* and *smoothly*.

For either to learn the movement (it's useful to the man, too), begin practice by lying on your back, knees up and feet flat on the floor. Now, slowly turn your tail so that the small of your back stays on the floor and the pubic area goes upward, toward the ceiling; then release and repeat. When this is done properly, the front muscles of the abdomen stay relaxed. Learn to rock your pelvis under you—the motion is the opposite of arching your back.

With the woman learning interesting movements for both partners' enjoyment, the man particularly needs that improved staying power. Neither person can benefit from the woman's delightful tricks if the man ejaculates the minute she uses them.

While "turning the tail under" is useful to a woman, it has even more value for the man. Commonly, in making sexual movements, a man holds his pelvis rigid, thereby tending to "hammer" his mate. "Turning the tail under" produces smooth, rocking motions—quite a different effect. We encourage both of you to practice this movement, first on your back to get the hang of it, then in any position you choose.

With the penis inside, the man can move in still closer, contract his p.c.g., then release it but *stay in deep*, shifting first to one side and then to the other. While slowly and gently moving the hips in a circle, he can turn the tail under and then release—very *slowly*, for maximum effect.

As a pleasantly satisfying contrast, try being quiet every so often. Lie there together with the vagina swallowing the deeply buried penis and the two of you being aware—experiencing! This is a nice time for the woman to contract her p.c.g. a few times, and the man can do the same, as if a ball were being tossed back and forth. She contracts, then he contracts.

Throughout, we have emphasized the need for slow movements and a slow enough pace to allow the development of internal feelings and awareness. The usual lovemaking session does not meet these needs, particularly when sexual hunger is present. A person who knows that food is available whenever he or she is ready for it can truly savor a meal, from hors d'oeuvres to dessert. For someone who is starving, the goal is to get hunger appeased, to wolf down the food *right now!*

A man who feels the pangs of sex hunger is unlikely to develop an appreciation for nuances. No appetizers: he wants the entree now! For the couple who wish to develop completeness in their sexual communication, an atmosphere of *sexual abundance* needs to be established, where sex is available wholeheartedly and cheerfully. Though there may be a difference in level of interest from time to time for either partner, the quiescent one can still enjoy the pleasure of giving.

Dorothy says, "Abundance is equally important for the woman. Without this certainty, which I truly have with Claude, I might not have happy, content feelings when I am quiescent and he is not."

We agree that the man needs freedom from that pressure which comes from the filling of the seminal vesicles, the little bladders that contain the male fluid. Sexual abundance will free him from that need to "empty himself" which precludes the kind of fulfilling sexual experience we've been discussing. On occasion, the woman, too, may experience a physiological pressure for which she needs an outlet. Either way, release from tension is needful.

Discuss sexual abundance together. Do you have this in your sex life? Did you in the past? What about your honeymoon? Is sexual abundance a new concept for one or both of you? In the discussion, share your feelings and thoughts. See if there have been ways you moved away from abundance (if you had it). Look for ways to move toward it. When a woman recognizes the need and provides for abundance, her partner will be more able and willing to provide the time and the attitude of leisure which make possible sexual fulfillment at a deeper level for both.

One way a woman can provide abundance is to encourage a "quickie" in the morning; then, in the evening, the man and woman can have the slow, long, satisfying experience. Or, a "quickie" early in the evening may lead to the main course later.

Claude observes, "When the planning calls for slow and languorous lovemaking and the trigger is pulled in spite of everything, then is when the warm and understanding attitude of the woman means so much. That happens to me too, and I truly am grateful for Dorothy's sincere 'Go ahead, enjoy it!' and her wholehearted appreciation of my experience."

When this happens the man can shorten the time for a repeat, *if his p.c.g. is in good tone,* by contracting it just before ejaculation commences. This restricts the amount of seminal fluid leaving the vesicles so that he "fills the tank" sooner. Some men find that semen retention heightens orgasmic intensity; others report the opposite.

Sexual scarcity, the opposite of abundance, can for either partner distort the implications of an affectionate gesture. The man's casual love pat, intended as a demonstration of affection, can generate tensions in the woman. She may withdraw from the caress because she's hung up on "what it means": that he wants to take her to bed, now or later. And, of course, she may be right. A "starving man" well may be sneaking a feel to see if there is a suggestion of relief in sight. On the other hand, she may have misinterpreted the situation.

In order to enjoy giving and receiving affection spontaneously, sharing it with no specifically sexual motives, both of you must be free of sexual hunger. You can find your own pattern of frequency. The woman who has the greater sexual drive, part of the time or mostly, may feel that there isn't "enough." When this happens she needs to have more lovemaking, which requires that the man be freed from the tyranny of the orgasm. He needs to understand that he can *enjoy* satisfying his wife's sexual needs without necessarily ejaculating each time. Discard the old notion that a man is harmed if he doesn't come; it's not true, and the thought itself can create physical tension. If he casts the idea aside, he'll have a pleasant glow instead.

Contracting the p.c.g. to limit semen discharge during ejaculation can increase his frequency without his feeling "pushed." Without this repatterning, he could fall into the kind of behavior one older man of a couple who consulted us experienced. He was not ready as often for sex as his wife. They both believed that he had to come, once they started, or it would be bad for his health. The man had developed a pattern of withdrawing from his wife, even shying away from affection, lest he be expected to "start something." Once they both changed their views, they were able to make love much more often. He ejaculated only when he felt ready; on other occasions he relaxed and enjoyed his pleasant sensuous reactions.

Sexual activity short of intercourse, eagerly sought and given during courtship, may become suppressed, distorted, or forgotten, and may produce anxiety years later. A "feel" may irritate the woman, rather than produce what the giver expects—a warm response. On the other hand, a common complaint we hear from women goes, "We used to do a lot of kissing and petting. Now we just seem to skip all that and grab a piece."

Dorothy says: "I can recall in our courtship times when I enjoyed creating and experiencing good, sexy feelings. It was fun to explore. The idea of orgasm wasn't present."

When our students were asked to look back at their courtship, some told us that they had more fun then. Fun! Even though many of them didn't have intercourse, much less an orgasm, they were experiencing themselves and each other. How much of this fun aspect is dropped with marriage? We think much of it is.

"When this happens," according to Claude, "it's as though every little action by the man is suspiciously looked at as an ominous signal, as though each must be on constant guard against the feelings of the other, or is it on guard against one's own feelings? For example, 'Oh, he's touching my fanny. Right now, I'm busy doing the dishes, but *that* means he wants me to go to bed with him.' Yet intimate touches during courtship probably were considered exciting by this same person and eagerly awaited. There is value in recovering that wholesome viewpoint.

"That pat on the fanny may mean the man wants to go to bed. On the other hand, it may just mean, 'You have a cute fanny—I like to pat it.' It could also mean, 'We don't make it together as often as we used to. I wish we could again.' "

If giving and receiving affection has gotten to be a loaded area for the two of you, try expressing your needs differently. Experiment with, "I'd like to hug (or kiss or touch) you for *right now*. Is that OK?" "I'd like to be close to you. I'd like you to hold me for just *right now*, is that okay?" Avoid "futurizing" your affection. Enjoy the moment, allowing your natural feelings to develop rather than pushing to have *or* not to have. When you agree on an experiment together, try to give the other as much "OKness" as you can.

Here is where communicating rather than assuming is useful. In addition, if both of you can talk with ease and comfort about what you *imagine* the other person has in mind, many areas of marital discord will be reduced.

The erosion of the courting-time affection may come slowly as the "new" wears off and each person begins to see the other as he or she is, not as each believed the other to be. One party or the other, in sexual matters and general living, may have had the suppressed thought: "I'll not fuss about this particular thing now, but after we're married I'll see to it that it's changed." This attitude almost seems to be unwritten courting custom in this country. Marriage is seen as the "license" to reform! Changes may come to pass all right when one person begins to push the "reform," but these are likely to be "negative" changes that drive a wedge between. True changes come from within, not from external pressure.

In courtship and in marriage, the mouth-to-mouth kiss is a vital expression of affection and desire. In our culture the kiss has different meanings for various situations. The kiss from the parent to the child differs from the kiss from child to child. Does a little girl kiss her father differently than she kisses her mother? Does a little boy kiss his mother differently than he kisses his father? There is the kiss from woman to woman. Not so often, in our culture, do we find the kiss from man to man.

Between mates, the hello kiss can be different from the little "I like you" peck or the casual goodbye kiss in the morning or the dramatic goodbye before an extended separation. In lovemaking, the kisses exchanged during the prelude are different from those exchanged after climax.

Implicit in the purpose of the kiss is the method. There is the tight-lipped kiss, the kiss with the lips puckered way out like "prunes," the kiss with the lips rolled out. Wet lips or dry lips? Not every person would agree as to which of these kisses is a "nice one," as opposed to one which isn't so nice.

The more passionate form of kiss, the open-mouth "French" type, can be done with the lips barely parted or comfortably wide open. The participation of the tongue offers opportunities for a variety of pleasurable sensations. The tongue may be used wherever it can reach, along the gums, the inside of the cheeks, the bottom or top of the mate's tongue.

Methods of kissing apply to caressing other parts of the body besides the lips. One can use the closed-mouth or the slack-mouth kiss on the nipples, the arms, the belly, back, buttocks, feet, hands, neck, fingers, and so on. How do you use your lips when you kiss your partner's body? In a variety of ways? When the man kisses his partner on the nipples, does he always hold his lips the same way? How does the woman kiss her partner's nipples, if at all? In the overall kissing experiment, did one or both of you try kissing and sucking on the toes, even nibbling? Receiving this caress can be exciting to both.

Kisses lit fires when you were courting. Their power is *still* available to generate passionate response.

EXPERIMENTS

1. Reliving Your Love Story

Reexperience how you found each other: review your beginnings together. How and when did you meet? What was your *first* reaction to each other? Did either or both of you have private thoughts that you've not yet shared? Be a little daring; see if you can unearth something new.

Did you notice some "faults" you hoped to change in the other person? Are they still present? If so, do you still see them as "faults"? Do you agree on this? Be cool on this one: don't put the other down. You're not trying to bend the other person out of shape!

Focus on your reactions to your mate's affection at that time—to kissing, touching, holding, cuddling.

If you had sex before marriage, see if there are additional feelings you can share now about that, one way or the other. The same applies if you didn't have sex before marriage. If either of you has been married before, do you have feelings of comparison you *avoid?* Just notice them.

2. Priceless Affection

Explore what you learned about affection from your mother and father. How do you feel about letting people know how you feel about them? Is it "safe" to let others see how you feel?

Recall and discuss times when you felt someone didn't accept your affection, times when someone did.

Examine your feelings and attitudes about giving and receiving affection *now*. If there have been changes, in what ways are they different now? Avoid criticism and accusation. Use the communication techniques given in Chapter Two.

Express what you *do* want from one another.

3. Kiss Me Again

Explore various ways of mouth-to-mouth and body kissing. Really let yourselves go. Try all the ways you've heard of and invent some new ones. The next time you come home after an evening out, stay in the car and "smooch."

4. Who's on First?

As you try a variety of positions, be aware of the varying sensations from one position to the next. Notice and discuss your mood and preferences about the positions. You need not try *all* of the positions in the next few days or even weeks. Save some for later stages of repatterning.

What positions allow each of you to move more freely? How do you feel about wiggling or squirming during lovemaking? Do you do it? Or do you avoid it? How do you feel about sexy movements? Find together what each of you thinks are sexy movements, in bed and out. Avoid re-evaluations for the other person. Appreciate how he or she "sees it."

If you don't have a book illustrating positions, explore face-to-face and face-to-back any position you've heard or read about and would like to try, or, invent some new ones. Use your imagination. Starting with the woman on top, see how many positions you can get into *without* taking the penis out.

5. Von Urban Position

The woman lies on her back with her knees raised until they touch her breasts.

The man lies at right angles to her, facing toward her buttocks, his penis at the entrance to her vagina.

The woman lowers her legs while the man places his upper leg *between* her legs.

The man then introduces his penis into her vagina.

As an alternate, the man may keep both legs together *beneath* the woman's legs.

6. Side-Scissors Position

Start with the man on top, penis inserted, and the woman's legs locked over the man's back. Gently tilt to one side. The man positions the woman's lower leg at his waist to minimize the pressure. This relaxed position permits a rich variety of movements and angles of entry —"until the woman's leg goes to sleep!" says Dorothy.

Or start with the man lying on his back. The woman sits on him, making penis entry, either facing toward or away from him with her legs out comfortably. Then tilt over to one side.

7. Rear-Entry Position

If either partner has resistance to rear entry, discuss this together. Was it the result of the first time you heard about it. Does the woman feel "too exposed"? Was there a time in the past when this position wasn't pleasurable?

If you decide to explore this position, talk about ways in which each of you can help the other. How can one partner make it easier for the other to enjoy this position? If you do enjoy it, talk about your feelings. Are there "special" times when you like using it? With what variations of the basic rear-entry position can you experiment?

6

The Sounds of Love

It is natural to express the joy and delight of lovemaking through love sounds; yet this is another area where it may take some doing to overcome childhood conditioning. Many men and women are embarrassed or too shy to make sounds during intercourse. Their worry, "What if someone should hear me?" may be another way of saying, "I can't let go this way." As one woman put it, "As long as sex was not really acceptable, neither were the sounds. I couldn't make them."

There is no more reason not to make sounds than there is reason not to make movement! The expression of love sounds can heighten a meaningful sexual experience. *Suppression* of sounds definitely places a limitation on one's total feeling of responsiveness.

Cultivate making the sounds of love, be they words or not; they help to let your partner know "where you are" and how you feel. Grunts, moans, groans, shouts, and screams are fine, as are vowel sounds (aiee, aaah, oooh, and so on).

As you practice the vowel sounds, notice how your tongue is used. It's important to relax the muscles in the floor of the mouth and the jaw. Dorothy believes this relaxation will be a reflection of the same "soft responsiveness" felt in the floor of the pelvis. By contrast, if the jaws are clenched and the lips are tight, that too can reflect in the pelvis as well and could result in tension there. You need not be slack-jawed every time you make a sound. But if you are often uptight in the mouth, try cultivating other patterning. Be aware of what happens within you when you resist making sounds you'd like to express.

In the beginning, producing love sounds despite your resistance may reduce sexual satisfaction because you may feel self-conscious. That seems as though you're going in the wrong direction. Be patient: as you overcome your feelings of resistance, the expansion of expression will take place.

Some people have reported that they feel stimulated when they *hear* the sounds of someone else's lovemaking. Have you ever been in a motel room and heard fervent moans and groans drifting through the wall? Did it turn you on? A little bit or a lot? If you didn't get started yourselves, did you have feelings or thoughts about making love right then?

One couple we know, after driving all day, checked into an old hotel. Being weary, they headed straight for bed and sleep. Through the paper-thin walls they could hear every sound of the love play going on in the next room. Our couple found themselves getting into the same mood and proceeded to some enthusiastic lovemaking of their own. As their passion died down, they heard giggles, then a voice saying, "I wonder if *they* heard *us!*" The woman in our couple said in a loud stage whisper: "We sure did, and it sounded great." There was a gasp from next door, followed by more giggling. These people would all agree no harm was done. Everybody enjoyed the listening and, perhaps, being listened to.

Practice and enjoy letting go with love sounds. If you feel funny about it, sing the vowel sounds in the shower (no one will notice) or during solo trips in the car, with the radio loud. Release the floor of the mouth and the jaw, with the tongue resting easy. When you're together, share your feelings about this.

Another area that needs desensitizing stems from an all-too-frequent childhood indoctrination: not only is sex "bad," but so are the parts of the body connected with sex. Somehow the "space between your legs" carried a stigma. It was "not nice," you shouldn't even think about it. All kinds of names may have been made up to describe the parts and what you did with them.

Dorothy explains her training: "When I was little, *that* space called 'down there' was treated as if it were separate from the rest of me, different—and, yes, bad. I was rigorously taught, after a bath, to dry my face first and 'down there' last, because 'it' was still dirty, even after a bath.

"It was not until the early days of our marriage, through Claude's expression of a loving attitude toward *all* of my body, that one part became just as nice to me as another. I was able, gradually, to accept his loving feelings toward my sex organs—in time I came to believe him when he said, 'You're *pretty* down there!' This led ultimately to my feelings of liking all of my body and all of it being part of me. Altering my attitude to where I feel *good* about the genital area has been a significant step for me, important in my coming to self-acceptance.

"I think that each woman needs to explore how she feels about her sex organs and the anal area, about 'how she is made.' "

Claude says, "My training was about the same. My penis was a 'fritzel' and my anus a 'bobo.' Whatever they were called, I was to avoid touching them when possible because they were 'unclean.' After holding my penis to urinate, my fingers felt as if they had invisible 'dirt,' which remained until I washed. So real was this belief that even as a young adult I imagined I could feel the difference between my fingers before and after the washing. It took time for me to work through this feeling."

When we have "ugh" feelings about any of the body parts in the pelvic region, the "not nice" overtones can dampen the positive feelings about sex that you're aiming to acquire. Even the names used for the body parts and the body products have their effect. What names did you use as a child? What do you use now? How do you really feel *inside*, when you say the words? Have you taught your children essentially the same things you were taught? If not, explore the differences.

In a similar vein is the question of sex during the menstrual period. Centuries-old cultural taboos notwithstanding, for some women this can be their most responsive time of the month! The old warnings about health dangers to either partner are unjustified. Actually, other than personal preference or prejudice, there is no reason not to make love during menstruation. One woman with a heavy flow solved *that* problem by making love with her husband in the shower.

Do you continue sexual contacts during menstruation? If not, have you wanted to or thought about it? Discuss your ideas and reactions.

The woman might remember her first menstrual period. What was she told about it beforehand? What was she taught about sex at that time, if anything?

What was the man told about menstruation? How did his mother (or sisters) act when having their period? What did he hear about having sex during menstruation?

Closely related to attitudes toward the body and its functions are the responses you have toward the words used to describe sexuality and subjects closely related— toward "four-letter words." How do you react to *cunt, cock, clit, ass, fuck, fart, shit, suck, blow, piss,* and any others with more or less four letters that apply? When you react to a word with a heightened negative response, be it disgust, defiance, or embarrassment, and when that reaction impedes the development of more positive feelings toward sexuality, then you would do well to "desensitize" that word.

We have found that members of our classes had doubts about the value of our desensitizing experiments —until they tried them!

The experience of a woman who came to America as a young adult is an interesting example. During the four-letter-word experiment she announced, with some degree of superiority, that she had no objections to the word *fuck*. We inquired what the equivalent was in her native language. She hesitated, obviously reluctant, then said, "When I say *that* word I feel uncomfortable. Now I know what you mean. *Fuck* is just a word to me but, well, *knülla*, that's different." She was asked to repeat this experiment in her native tongue until she felt comfortable about the words.

To help desensitize yourselves, face each other, preferably nude, and say all the four-letter words you can remember for body parts, functions, and products. Should you find a word that particularly bothers you, imagine that you are a child and say the word aloud a few times from that viewpoint. Shift to pretending from the viewpoint of an adult, then a parent. Be aware of any difference in your responses as you shift from the child to the adult viewpoints. Continue the experiment until the word becomes a collection of sounds, "just another word."

Some couples confess they have suppressed a wish to use four-letter words, now and then, during their love-making. Releasing inner reactions to these words allows more freedom to express feelings that run deeper than "refined" words can convey. The use of the words during Sexual Repatterning can provide another way of getting in touch with gut-level responses.

EXPERIMENTS

1. Whooping It Up!

Talk about your attitudes toward love sounds and making them.

If it is agreeable to both, make love and let the sounds come out!

2. What Did You Call It?

Remember and share as many words as you can that were used in your family to describe penis, vagina, breasts, nipples, scrotum, clitoris, buttocks, bowel movements, flatus, urine and urination, anus, sexual arousal, sexual climax. What terms do you use now?

Do you have your own pet names for sex organs and actions? Would you like to invent some? Discuss this together.

3. Turning on Four-Letter Magic

Do the four-letter-word desensitizing described on page 90 as many times as necessary to clear this area.

There are other four-letter words such as love, hold, kiss, care, to mention only a few. See what happens when you voice these words with the inflection and attitude conventionally used to express the earthy four-letter types.

4. How Does He or She Pee?

We'd like you to explore a common body process. Children often wonder how a member of the opposite sex, having different apparatus, urinates. Parental attitudes tend to drive this curiosity underground, yet we have found that this childhood curiosity can still be present many years later.

The woman is to accompany her husband to the toilet when he needs to urinate, and she is to hold his penis for him and direct the stream. Women have expressed a variety of reactions, including amusement, pleasant satisfaction, and pride in "hitting the mark." One woman, with several males in her family, reported enlightenment after she had difficulty aiming the stream. She decided she would not be so critical of her boys when cleanup around the toilet was necessary.

To satisfy the man's curiosity about "what goes on down there," the woman can spread her legs wide, or she can lie in the bath tub, knees up and spread apart so that he can *really* see!

5. The Throne Room

Discuss your feelings about bathroom activities.

Is it OK for him/her to be in the room?

Are you embarrassed about toilet sounds and smells? Do you run the water or flush the toilet while you urinate? When did you start that?

Do you read on the toilet? If you do, set the reading material aside and try experiencing *what* you're doing on the toilet. Notice your reactions.

Do you use the bathroom as a getaway space? Do you *have* to lock the door or not? Consider that privacy is better based upon a preference than a compulsion.

7

Looking: Inside and Out

From our childhood we are taught how impolite it is to stare at other people, and watching their erotic activity is taboo to say the least. The slightest interest in watching is suspect. And yet, given the chance to look, the average person's *willingness* to look is undeniable. The reason is simple. Listening to other people's lovemaking can be sexually stimulating; so can watching.

Have you ever accidentally been the audience for a couple in the throes of passion? Perhaps they didn't draw their blinds; perhaps they were busy in the woods when you stumbled upon them. Were you tempted to watch? If so, did you? Have you ever talked about watching with your partner? Explore your memories or fantasies together.

On the other hand, was there ever a time when you realized *you* were being watched? If so, how did you feel about that? Were you simply embarrassed, or was there any enjoyment in being observed? If you did enjoy it, that's not surprising. It's natural to take pride in performing well, whatever the activity.

"Looking" curiosity can take many forms. Just what do the woman's labia, vulva, etc. look like when the penis is moving in and out? Satisfying that curiosity can be stimulating to both the man and the woman.

A kneeling rear-entry position offers the man a good view, but both partners can enjoy the looking experience if the man slowly introduces and withdraws a substitute for his penis—a vibrator, cucumber, banana, or whatever is available. If a mirror is used, the woman can see herself more clearly. And, being hostess to a penis substitute can be a highly erotic form of love play or, now and then, a sexual contact that is satisfying in itself.

A large mirror permanently or temporarily positioned near your bed is sure to reflect interesting views. A mirror on the ceiling is something else again! The connoisseur may use several mirrors, placed at angles so that different perspectives are possible.

How do you feel about watching each other make love in this way? Have you ever tried it? If not, have you *thought* about trying it? Discuss your responses, whatever they may be.

Looking need not necessarily be sexual, even assuming both partners are nude at the time. Just being together, naked, can promote a relaxed, barriers-down feeling: you can't hide behind clothes you aren't wearing! When appropriate, both of us enjoy various activities in the nude, many of them nonsexual: reading, eating, visiting together, or doing chores, to mention only a few. We enjoy seeing each others' bodies freed from the restraints of clothing, and may not find the experience at all sexually arousing.

The point is not, in fact, to arouse. Whether sexual arousal does or does not take place, there is warmth and enjoyment in looking at the other's nude body with no hesitancy or embarrassment.

That can't happen, of course, until the conventional conditioning that sexual organs are "bad" is overcome. If you feel you need to be freed from such conditioning, try exploring the way each of you feels about the appearance of the genitals—in general, and yours or your partner's in particular.

Consider the shape. Do they remind you of something attractive, appealing, or enticing? Look at your partner's genitals with an eye to seeking out beauty or appeal. As you do this, discuss together your reactions. If negative responses turn up, discuss where you might have learned such reactions and how you might help each other set them aside.

As you become more accepting and appreciative of each other's bodies, more opportunities for mutual pleasure emerge. You might try being nude together under various types of lighting: candlelight, moonlight, the light from an open fire. Or, you may find that seeing each other very clearly in full, strong light is best.

As your pleasure at seeing your partner in the nude develops, you may begin to experience the clothed person differently. The outline of nipples beneath the woman's blouse, the bulge in the man's trousers, the shadow of the woman's vaginal cleft all can become reminders of the other's body, a source of pleasant association.

The difference between the male and female genital structure ensures that the woman's sexual apparatus seems more mysterious, the man's more obvious. *His* is right there for her to see—the size of the penis, the shape of the glans and testicles, and so on. Not so for the man. The woman's pubic hair may prevent him from seeing even the opening he's going to put his penis into, much less what lies within. On some deep level he may fear what lies inside—or, at the least, he may assume "it" to be unappealing if not dreadful-looking.

The man who actually looks inside his partner's vagina is likely to be in for a pleasant surprise. In our classes, we've given a plastic speculum to each couple so they could take it home and enjoy the ultimate looking experience. With speculum, flashlight, and mirror (so *she* can look, too), they explore together and almost invariably find this a fascinating, mutually gratifying experience.

"After looking inside my wife," one man said, "I feel as though I 'know' her for the first time. It's lovely in there ... warm and pink and welcoming." Another man had always felt that his wife's vagina was unclean, like a wound. Subconsciously, he had responded during love-making as if he were putting himself into raw flesh. The actual look inside freed him from the inhibitions his notions had created, and this couple's lovemaking benefitted dramatically as a result.

There are men who become quite taken with the pink color they find inside, the particular "corner" that feels so good, the ridges they've felt with their fingers, the bulgy shape of the cervix, with its pink dimple, that dominates the whole area. Others really enjoy the pools of "juice." And there are women who love to be looked at inside just as much as their partner enjoys the looking!

Some couples explore the anal cavity as well, which is fine assuming both the man and woman are interested. The textures and colors are different from those in the vagina: the surface is smoother, the color much deeper. The woman, too, may be interested in seeing how her partner looks inside.

EXPERIMENTS

1. Let's See...

If you can obtain a speculum from your physician or pharmacist, practice opening and closing it before putting it to use. Then, using ample lubrication, introduce it (closed!) into the vagina or anus, gently and slowly. Your partner can comment if it seems at all uncomfortable. When opening and closing the speculum inside, so you can look, do it slowly.

Even without a speculum, you can make use of your fingers and a flashlight to "see" more of your partner than you ever saw before.

2. Mirror, Mirror

Experiment with setting up mirrors in your bedroom so that you can watch, from various angles, your love-making. Try keeping your eyes closed until penetration, or until orgasm is impending, then open them and watch. Or, try watching the whole procedure, beginning to end.

3. So That's How It Looks

If the idea appeals to both of you, experiment with the man looking as he inserts a substitute penis into the woman's vagina. What are your reactions—excitement, shyness, satisfaction, stimulation? Share both ways, fully.

8

Masturbation:
Solo and Duo

Our cultural attitudes have strongly disapproved of masturbation by children or adults—or have at least until the current generation. Few of us are free of parental conditioning in this regard; most adults have residual hang-ups. For the most part, we all were reared in an atmosphere that considered any form of childhood sexual curiosity or activity "wrong": childhood exploration had to be carefully hidden, conducted in silence and secrecy, lest one be caught.

The effect of this can be seen in adult lovemaking: the rush to orgasm, the embarrassed reluctance to discuss sex, the repression of hearty sexual responsiveness. The childhood need to conceal not only the activity but even the *thought* of sex surfaces in the adult who tries to hide his or her responses even from the sexual partner, the one person with whom it is essential to be most open!

We believe masturbation can have a place in sexual sharing between two mature adults. It can also be a healthy form of self-expression when sexual activity between the man and woman is not possible. Even though people in general may still tend to frown upon masturbation, studies show that over half the adult women and nearly all adult men masturbate at some time. With the array of "sensuous" books that have appeared over the last couple of years, one might even get the idea that there's something wrong with you if you don't masturbate!

Examine your attitudes toward the word *masturbation*, especially as applied to lovingly caressing your partner's genitals. Do you have an "OK" or an "ugh" feeling? Your answer may be an indication of how much you are still responding to earlier patterning.

Masturbating can help you learn how feelings and sensations develop—for the woman, how her sensations transfer from the outside to the inside; for the man, how to detect more accurately the signals that say he is close to ejaculation so that he can practice *when* to slow down or wait.

The use of masturbation as a learning process to help a woman generate strong sexual feelings has been widely mentioned in the past few years. Getting to know what orgasmic feelings are like will give the sexually inhibited woman the confidence that she *can* experience them during intercourse; and, we add, she will be able to recognize the beginnings and allow them to build.

It's important that the movements used in masturbation be slow. Rapid rubbing, and especially stimulation with a vibrator, may well be ineffective. A woman should develop her arousal with *slow* movements and transfer this learning to sexual intercourse; a man who masturbates rapidly is establishing poor sexual patterns too.

From the woman's point of view, Dorothy says, "If a vibrator is used, begin away from the specific genital area. Stimulate the inside of the thighs, the lower abdomen, the pubic mound, slowly moving toward the labia. Then follow the fundamental repatterning instructions we have given for transfer of the sensations from the clitoris to the vagina (see page 47). As with the penis, move slowly, ten strokes per minute, with infrequent—or no—use of the motor.

"We found that batteries that are nearly worn out work better because they slow the vibrations and create a slower-faster operation, which by its unpredictability heightens sensual response.

"For a woman who has not had even a clitoral climax, the use of a vibrator, for a while, can be a help. After getting the feel of it she should concentrate on developing her independent responses, using slow movements with her fingers or the quiet vibrator. If she *depends* upon the vibrator she will not be helping her cause."

Stimulation of areas not specifically genital may intensify response during masturbation. This can take the form of fondling or stroking erogenous zones, nipples or breasts, possibly the anal region. There is a relatively common male practice of introducing fingers or objects into the anus to heighten response or to provide, of itself, pleasurable sensations. Women too may use anal stimulation to good effect. One woman used two syringes, one for her vagina and the other for her anus. As she came to climax she released the clamps on the tubes to flood both cavities and intensify her orgasm.

Another pleasurable technique is to play or spray a stream of water onto the genital area. This can be done by lying in the tub, legs raised and spread apart. Allow the warm water to splash from the faucet onto the responsive areas. This is easier if you have a shower attachment with an adjustable spray feature which produces a more concentrated stream of water. For a woman, rhythmic movement with the water stream can provide an orgasmic response that can be deeply satisfying, an entirely different experience from "ordinary" masturbation. The water stream can also be used as a mutually stimulating activity before a man and woman have intercourse.

Discuss your attitudes and reactions to these practices, whether they seem exciting or awful. Notice your objections, if any. When you and your partner have reevaluated viewpoints, tell each other about any adult masturbation experience—how it felt, what was nice or what was not so nice.

Before making love, or even as an experience unto itself, caressing the genitals of your partner is a normal, natural way to express your affection and excitement toward each other.

When the woman is receiving her husband's finger caresses, telling him what feels good *and where* is appropriate. She could even reach over and guide his fingers. At the clitoris, does his finger tip feel better on the left or the right? Is it best right at the tip? Would it be better if he moved away and then came back? Is a firm pressure at the root enjoyable? The man can help transfer the woman's feelings to the inside by moving from the clitoral area slowly down the valley and into the vagina.

For the woman: in the vagina, do you like one finger or more? touching one area or moving around? the back wall or the front? shallow or deep? Let him know your wishes.

Communicate!

For the man: gently lift the labia with the clitoris between and roll all softly between finger and thumb. As a woman becomes more responsive through Sexual Repatterning she is likely to prefer slow clitoral stimulation. She may move her hips eagerly but still want the finger movement to be *slow.*

Men and women differ in their responses to stimulation of sexual zones. While men tend to rush in, women generally respond more favorably to indirect caressing of the surrounding areas first and then a gentle homing in on the target.

A man may know this at the intellectual level and use this knowledge in the beginning of a relationship with a woman but slip into a more abrupt approach with time. He acts as if "that's no longer necessary," which is the wrong approach.

Dorothy expresses it this way: "A woman can experience abrupt movements as a 'personal violation,' especially when that's the *only* approach she receives. Certainly there can be times when more vigorous activity is desired. But generally a woman prefers to be caressed rather than rubbed on the erogenous zones."

Communication is just as useful when the woman is caressing the man. Try beginning with light touches, barely brushing the hairs on legs and belly; then, if he wants it, try stronger contact. Use slow strokes in the crevice between his legs and scrotum. Gently cup and tenderly message his testicles. Use light finger-tip strokes behind the scrotum. On the penis, the rim of the head deserves attention, as does the opening. When you are stroking his penis, circle it with your fingers; using lubrication (saliva is ideal), move slowly over the rim of the glans on the upstroke.

As a man progresses with his Sexual Repatterning there may be times when he enjoys the genital caressing without the usual arousal symbol: a "full-mast" erection. If this happens, it does *not* mean that he isn't enjoying and appreciating the attention, assuming he can accept how he feels at that time.

Once the no-no's of masturbation have been laid to rest, personal genital caressing may now and then become a part of lovemaking. Occasionally a woman enjoys the combination of sensations produced by her man's penis inside while she strokes her clitoris as they are in a rear-entry or Von Urban position or when she's astride him. She may continue on to climax or taper off as her arousal indicates. Many a man reports that knowing—and especially seeing (when she's astride)—that his mate is caressing her body provides a curious but powerful thrill, a heightening of sensual feelings.

The man may derive the same enjoyment from watching his wife stroke her genitals during the prelude; and the woman may feel arousal upon watching her partner fondle his penis.

Allowing yourselves the freedom to touch and be touched is an important step to accepting your body and yourself, as is accepting self-touching in your partner. We have encountered women who showed concern about noticing that their husbands fondled themselves while lying in bed. As one woman expressed it, "I couldn't believe my eyes. He was *playing* with himself!" She felt there must be something wrong with him. After some reassurance from us she tried a new response. The next time it happened, she said, "Hey, can I get in on the act too?" His response was, "*What* act?" As they discussed the situation, his wife realized that to him the fondling was not specifically sexual, just comforting and soothing. As far as he was concerned, he was thinking about closing a real-estate deal!

Need we emphasize again the importance of communication?

EXPERIMENTS

1. Talk about It

Explore and discuss your reactions, your feelings about masturbation, personal and mutual.

What were you told about it as a child? Do you remember when you first heard about masturbation? Did you do it before you heard of it? Did you ever get caught? What were the consequences? When did you first masturbate to climax? How did you feel afterward?

Can you see ways in which these childhood or teenage experiences and feelings could be monitoring your sexual patterns now? If you don't like being so influenced, what can you do about it now?

In Chapter Two we asked you to examine and discuss your childhood sexuality. Please do so again, using this material as a basis. Also look into the teen-age years.

2. Masturbation, Anyone?

The next time you wake up in a state of even slight sexual arousal, don't wake your partner. Instead, masturbate to climax. If he or she wakes up and notices, that's fine.

Another time, deliberately masturbate to climax while your partner watches you. Then masturbate your partner to climax.

Masturbate to climax, and then, *later,* if both of you are in the mood, make long, slow love with your partner.

Create your own subexperiments, trying out whatever combination of masturbation and intercourse occurs to you.

3. Trading Places

During a prolonged kiss, agree to place all your attention into your own lips, then into your partner's, then back into your own. Be aware of and share together what each of you experiences. Repeat at other times when you kiss, without telling your partner beforehand. Share afterward.

9

Oral-Genital Love

In the last few decades our society has undergone drastic changes in every area—social, economic, racial, political, you name it. Sexual attitudes have been changing too, and for many of us reared according to earlier codes these changes have been difficult to face, let alone accept. Our conditioning is not easy to drop. It doesn't change simply because the law changes or because people speak more freely.

The release from old hang-ups requires a deconditioning and a reconditioning, the essence of Sexual Repatterning. The goal is to feel, down in one's core, that whatever a loving couple agree to and enjoy doing together is what is proper to do. The fact that a particular society, at a particular time, has labeled certain sexual acts as perverted does not necessarily mean that these practices are anything of the kind.

We get a clearer focus on this when we look at other cultures and see that what is "right" here can be "wrong" there. In pre-World War II Japan, mouth-to-mouth kissing was taboo. In parts of India today, a woman with both breasts covered is assumed to be a prostitute. In one part of the world, eating is considered a disgusting spectacle, to be conducted in private, as we treat defecation. In another, a male visitor naturally sleeps with the wife of the household. And the list could go on!

What is important is your own personal views on sexuality, arrived at together. Ask yourself how you can bring more pleasure to each other, how you can become still closer. Potentially the sexual act can bring two people as close as it is possible to be. In such cobeingness lies the shared awareness that can make life rewarding, fulfilling for each of you.

During the transports of the sexual experience the man and woman tune in on the same vibrations, share an extraordinary closeness. But if there are reservations about what is proper, if certain acts are considered shameful, it can be impossible to achieve this deep intimacy.

Talk about your reservations. Talk about the things you would like to do but haven't dared. Recognize that other people may feel the same inhibitions. We see couples who have been married for years without the man's kissing his wife's nipples. We say that kissing her nipples is fine, and her vagina too, if they both like that, to say nothing of her fanny, her toes, or anything else that happens to strike his fancy and hers. It works the other way, too. The woman can find exciting areas to stimulate with her lips and her tongue as well as her finger tips.

An area in which many people have hang-ups involves the sense of smell. A normal male can enjoy the odors of his sexual partner. But *can* he, if he has reservations about kissing her genital area? If he feels that it's bad or perverted, his basic male sensuousness may not be stirred. He misses that really gutsy level of himself. Actually, the vaginal secretions of the beloved woman who is aroused have a musky perfume that is quite special. Unhappily, some men are so conditioned that they do not recognize, or acknowledge, this subtlety.

With all oral-genital contacts, proper hygiene is imperative. Odors can develop with lack of care—the smell of stale urine or old smegma *is* abhorrent—but the healthy genital area does not generate unpleasant odors of itself. If showering or bathing took place long before lovemaking, an extra washing of the genital area before making love is a good idea for man or woman.

If your bathroom has a bidet, wonderful. That's the best possible washbasin for your genitals and bottom. Since few American homes have them, here is an alternate method. Whether you are male or female, seat yourself on the toilet, facing the tank, with your legs spread wide. You need a small pitcher of warm water, mild soap, and a hand towel. Pour a portion of the water over the outer genital area; add a light layer of soap. Cupping one hand under you, pour more of the water into the palm and guide it to the genital and anal areas. Move the hand up and down, from front to back, to complete the washing and rinsing. (Remember, the hair needs washing too.) Towel the water off, and you're ready for whatever the sexual contact may bring.

We don't recommend the spray-type genital deodorants or chemically treated "wipe offs." Some women have experienced painful swelling of the labia after their use. Plain, mild soap and water will provide freedom from odor for a healthy body. (When it's feasible, women can allow the vagina to "breathe" by leaving off panties or panty hose.) If even with these measures strong odors persist, a visit to your physician is indicated.

What about douching? Well, the flavored and scented varieties certainly suggest that oral-genital "fun" is being acknowledged by the manufacturers! However, to be serious many doctors agree that the average woman douches entirely too frequently. Washed away are the woman's natural protective juices; left is a scarcity of the secretions that should accompany sexual arousal. The douche is indicated to meet a special, usually temporary condition and is to be done, ideally, upon a doctor's recommendation. Otherwise, use mild soap and water, *outside!*

The relationship between smells and sexual attraction in insects and animals has long been established. Substances called *pheromones* secreted by females are the attractant for the male. Studies in the last few years indicate that a similar linkage in the human animal may exist.

While no conclusive proof has yet been established, researchers speculate that the daily shower with soap may be making women *less* sexy by destroying their natural sex-attractant odors.

Too much hygiene can be a disadvantage. In one of our classes a man commented that he liked to experience his wife's womanly smell, her own "perfume," during their lovemaking. She felt that when he showed any signs of ardor, she should hurry to the shower. After some discussion, she was convinced that he preferred her perfume to the elegant scent of her bath soap.

Women may get the idea that there must be something wrong with their husbands if they like to smell them. Dorothy says, "It's important for a woman to understand that she can smell good, that she can generate a lovely perfume in her vagina." By accepting this she will be able to enjoy being experienced by her partner in this way, rather than accepting it passively.

The bodily juices of the normal, healthy, loved woman not only smell good, they may taste good to her partner. Consequently we consider oral-genital contacts (cunnilingus and fellatio) normal, proper, right, healthy—and delightful.

Cunnilingus is hardly a twentieth-century creation. There are documentary and pictorial records of oral-genital loving from Greece, Rome, India, China, Japan, and Bali. The sex songs of the Letts, dating back four or five thousand years, are enthusiastic about its special pleasures and prehistoric cave paintings depict couples enjoying mutual oral-genital caresses.

European attitudes toward oral-genital love have been more natural than in the United States and Great Britain. France has even contributed the term "Frenching" for oral-genital loving. In America it is being practiced more frequently, even if still furtively. We find that once couples accept the idea of oral love as "all right," their suppressed wish to try it often emerges.

The experience told us by an older man illustrates a fairly common reaction to the first oral-genital affection. "When I was about twenty, I remember that during a loving time with my girlfriend I had the impulse to kiss her genitals. I'd not done that before, but I tried it. She looked at me and said, 'What a funny place to kiss me!'"

Reluctance toward oral-genital love can often be traced to school locker-room experience. Scornful comments about "cunt lapping"—"no nice girl does that or lets anyone do it to her"—may well be the stumbling block to a mature sexual experience.

Claude recalls an incident in which a man who had been going out with a young woman seemed altar-bound until this episode occurred: "They were busy with some amorous activities in his car. He had a hand up her skirt and she was fondling him, when suddenly she took his penis in her mouth. He told me he was through with her. He couldn't bear the idea of being in love with a perverted woman!"

Consider the cultured Scandinavian woman who had a hang-up the other way around. While driving in a secluded area, she and her escort parked for a while. With his finger manipulating her clitoris, she had a powerful orgasm. She undid his zipper, took his penis in her mouth, and brought him swiftly to climax. Then she commented that she much preferred the "mouth thing" to the "regular." "All that rapid moving and sweating—ugh! I don't like it. This is so much nicer."

Either extreme can interfere with full sexual expression, can suppress the meaningful flow of loving feelings between the loving couple.

Kissing, licking, or sucking the genital area can be a prelude to intercourse or it can be the whole experience, depending upon what the two of you want at the time. Bringing your partner to orgasm by this means can be a thrilling experience. Is it all right for the man to ejaculate in his wife's mouth? Why not, if that's what both would like?

In class, one woman asked if the man's semen would be poisonous to her. She was really serious! Heaven knows where she had come by *that* misinformation. After discussion, she decided to try it and found it far from poisonous. As she put it, "He tastes good!"

For most women, it requires practice to take the man's penis in the mouth without gagging. One woman who had never tried it before attempted to accept deep penetration and ejaculation the first time. In her enthusiasm, she was trying to take his entire penis deeply into her mouth, and her gag reflex was triggered. Fortunately, they both treated it as a joke. It would be better, the first time you try fellatio, just to lick and kiss. Another time, take the penis into the mouth with some gentle sucking, which may lead, at still another time, to accepting ejaculation—if *both* of you want it.

With practice, some women learn to overcome gagging, some do not. And so it is the woman who should control the penetration to allow only as much as is comfortable for her. This is something to consider ahead of time. Should the man become overly stimulated, the woman can encircle his penis with her fingers so that she can restrict how deep it goes.

Whether or not the man ejaculates in the woman's mouth should, again, be *her* decision. If she has doubts, talk about them first.

If ejaculation *is* decided upon, we advise the woman not to point the penis toward the throat the first time. Instead, direct the head of the penis into the cheek pouch and allow the ejaculation to occur there. Some women like to keep extra saliva in the mouth to dilute the fluid if its taste is not pleasant to them. What is done with the ejaculate, whether it is swallowed or not, once again is the woman's decision. A man need not have "funny" feelings if the woman prefers not to swallow it.

Recognize that attitudes can change *spontaneously* from within the person and a prior decision may be canceled. The woman who "thinks" she wouldn't even want to take the penis in her mouth may decide later she'd like to try it. She may even decide she'd like to go the whole way and have her husband come in her mouth.

As Dorothy sees it: "I think it's important for a woman

to follow her feelings, her impulses, *especially* in oral-genital love. A woman may decide, ahead of time, that she wants her husband to come in her mouth, but then, at the crucial moment, chicken out. This is OK. Or the woman may tell him, 'I just want to hold your penis in my mouth, I don't want you to come,' but then she feels so good about loving it that, on impulse, she changes her mind and encourages him to come. These things are hard to decide ahead of time. A woman must trust her spontaneous desires."

The husband needs to be sensitive and understanding toward his wife's inner needs and wishes on these occasions, to tune in on the message conveyed by her movements and gestures. A woman is likely to feel more vulnerable if she is being held too tightly at these times. It's impossible for her to hear her partner when his hands are over her ears, much less answer with a penis in her mouth! The man would do better to stroke her hair and face to express his appreciation.

For those who are uninitiated in oral-genital experiences, the ideal positions would be those which allow the woman to have the freedom to move and control her own head and neck movements. This also applies to mutual oral loving. We are reminded of the man who commented that he couldn't hear, much less answer, his wife because her favorite position was to wrap her legs tightly around his head.

The woman's tongue can be a delightful instrument for stimulating the penis: along the shaft, on the glans, in the opening, over the scrotum, around the base—you choose it! Changing from firmness to delicacy can add to the variety of sensations for the man.

As a prelude to mouth stimulation of the penis, the woman may start by kissing and licking along the lower portion of the abdomen. Next, still avoiding the genital area, move to the upper thighs, spread the legs and continue the caresses upward on the inner surfaces. Gently taking the man's testicles into her mouth and rolling them around with her tongue provides a rather special sensation all by itself for both partners. And moist fingers or tongue caressing the base of the scrotum can produce intense pleasure.

Ideally the woman delays taking the penis into her mouth. Instead she teases the shaft with her tongue, nibbling or biting with her lips covering her teeth, licking with the tongue flattened and then pointed. She should provide enough saliva to create a slippery feeling. Use slow movements, stopping just to hold or otherwise caress the penis.

For many women, the first kiss on the tip of the penis is the real beginning of the oral loving. Some report a special excitement at sucking gently the first drop of the man's fluid. Licking motions are best on and around the head of the penis. Gradually accept more of the glans as the loving progresses. A woman's holding on with a sucking action while shaking her head can provide added stimulation for her partner. She may encourage thrusting movements, if she likes, by moving her husband's hips toward and away from her. He picks up his cues from her.

When the man is to give the oral-genital caress, the same sort of circuitous path is best: abdomen, thighs, inner thighs, buttocks, labia. Extending the preliminaries, delaying the actual oral-genital caress by kissing and licking and nibbling, adds excitement and anticipation. Saving the clitoral area for the last can be nice! Even then, don't give initial emphasis to the clitoris; working along on either side is better. Try probing with the pointed tongue into the vagina. Draw the labia outward by sucking on them. Gentle sucking on the clitoris can produce intense sensations. With exploration, the man can find the opening of the urethra and attempt to insert the very tip of his tongue into it. That isn't possible, of course, but the circular, pointed tongue movements can be exciting. As a variation, while making the tongue broad and flat, lap the whole area in slow strokes from back to front. Try side-to-side strokes too. Use fingers to hold the labia open.

At those times during intercourse when the man climaxes before his partner, going down on her while a finger or two is inserted in her vagina can bring her to orgasm too. Ideally, the mouth caresses should *not* be delayed while she washes away ejaculate: the interruption can be a heavy damper. However, a man may not want to put his mouth in contact with his own semen. He needs to see how he feels about this. The woman may also be uncomfortable with the thought. We recommend that you discuss your feelings. The man might try tasting a little to find out how he reacts. He may discover that you taste good "together."

Oral loving requires taking a good look at how you feel

about using your sense of taste and of smell. By experiencing each other in a different way you become more aware of yourself—your feelings, resistances, beliefs. Unspoken thoughts can be more powerful than spoken words. Be aware of your reactions as you read, be they good, bad, or indifferent. We're not asking you to change them—just notice.

EXPERIMENTS

1. Oral-Genital Love

Discuss your ideas of oral-genital contacts, whether or not these contacts are usual or unusual for you. If you can't even consider discussing oral-genital contacts, *talk about that.* For example, you might talk about your reactions when you first found out that partners kissed each other's genitals. Or about the words you have heard to describe this practice and how you feel about them.

Discuss any specific reactions you have to our suggestions.

Use the sharing communication techniques given on pages 23–24. Remember to avoid attempts to change the other person's view. An appropriate response to a communication, even if you heartily disagree with it, can be something like, "I hear you. I'm having trouble agreeing."

2. Going Down—in Style

If oral-genital love is new for you, help each other in whatever ways you can to explore together; share your desires, get acquainted, take your time.

If oral-genital love is not new for you, try slower movements and a longer buildup with mouth, lips, and tongue *before* caressing the genitals. Try a new position.

3. Cuddling

Lie side by side, quietly, with as much skin contact as possible for a while, then reverse sides. This doesn't mean you are to be stiff as boards. Small movements to improve comfort from time to time are all right. Try facing in the same direction to provide front-to-back contact.

This is to be an intense *feeling* experience. Be aware of what passes between your bodies. As Kahlil Gibran put it: "Lovers embrace that which is between them rather than each other."

4. Quietly Inside

After choosing a comfortable side-to-side position, enter the penis into the vagina with little preliminary lovemaking.

Lie together, being aware of each other and of what passes between you.

The erection may subside; no matter. If you prefer the continuance of the erection, one or the other of you can contract the p.c.g. muscle or make small bodily motions, for a short time, to maintain it. However, erection is not essential. Nobody comes during *this* one. Just be aware of one another.

Share your feelings, your impressions, your objections, your satisfactions, your pleasures.

5. Repatterning Practice for the Woman

Hold the man's penis and use it to stroke from the clitoris into the vagina, always moving toward the goal of feeling "good" sensations inside, too. (Check back to page 47.)

10

Anal Love

Writing this chapter on anal loving brought us face to face with some of our own hang-ups. Dorothy's initial reaction was: "That settles it. I want to write under an assumed name!" Her second was: "How about just skipping this chapter?"

We discussed our options and reviewed our teaching experiences. We considered the possibility that no matter *what* we said about anal loving, some would consider this to be a "dirty book" after all. Putting the pieces together, we still felt the subject was part of the total picture we were emphasizing, especially since most marriage manuals ignore anal sexuality or give strong admonitions against it. A few present a slightly positive attitude. We have yet to find a book with a comprehensive, honest discussion of "how to" for the couple who may wish to explore this area of lovemaking; yet anyone can go to an "adult" bookstore and find porny novels dealing explicitly with anal activity in a sadomasochistic manner. How sad if the only instruction available to a loving couple were from such a source! We took our courage pills and decided that an open and complete discussion of anal love *is* appropriate.

Dorothy adds the woman's viewpoint: "It has been our experience that the couple who is not informed and 'does it anyway' will be more likely to have an unfortunate, painful experience, or a break in their feelings and communication with each other. As a result, a permanent KEEP OUT sign may be erected, which means that each time the husband's hand wanders 'too close' the woman becomes tense. This can affect their lovemaking even though the man may have had no intention whatsoever of touching her anus at that time."

For most people, the anus is associated with bowel functions and is therefore considered "dirty," to be avoided. This attitude could mean losing an opportunity for interesting, pleasurable, satisfying experience. As with other bodily orifices, the anus is rich in nerves and is capable of responding strongly to sensual stimulation.

Usually the man is assumed to be the one interested in anal intercourse, presumably because of his desire for a "tighter fit" than that provided by the vagina. Our teaching experience does not match that view. About twenty percent of the women in our classes have expressed interest in, or curiosity about, or have experimented with anal sexual activity. Our own data, supported by recent published information, suggest that anal intercourse can be of specific and definite interest to many women, after they have freed themselves from "cultural hang-ups."

One of the concerns expressed by men or women contemplating anal activity is the possibility of encountering fecal matter if the anal play goes inside the rectum. Actually, the rectal structure is so made that, following the bowel movement, there should be no residue.

Two sphincters control the action. The upper sphincter closes and moves down to expel the bowel movement as the lower opens. When the activity is finished, the upper sphincter moves back to its normal location, about six inches above the anus. There is little likelihood of encountering fecal matter provided the anal play is conducted after a needed bowel movement has been completed. If you have an effective p.c.g. muscle, you can recognize the presence of material in the lower bowel more readily, and you are more likely to have a complete evacuation.

If you and your partner become interested in anal activity, and you sense feces could be present, visit the toilet. Then use the pitcher douche technique mentioned on page 113, and you're ready.

"All right," you say, "suppose I do get bold and try this and my finger does encounter some? What do I do then?" In the event that this does occur, you have several choices. You can stop and wash your hands. You can ask your partner to visit the toilet. You can ignore the whole thing. After all, a few hours ago it was food!

The anus is, after all, the other end of the mouth. Sound strange? Try thinking of it that way. The mouth is a nice place to kiss and so is the other end of the mouth —assuming it's clean. If someone has bad breath, mouth kissing isn't going to be pleasant either. The same applies to anal kisses (analingus). An educated young Western European expressed the idea thus: "If I love someone, I love everything about her. Nothing about my partner is unclean or undesirable. Rimming [analingus] is a way of demonstrating this."

What makes anal kisses attractive and enjoyable? For the receiver, there are intense, pleasurable sensations. Men say arousal and erection are strengthened. Women say vaginal secretions are stimulated, and the proper "mood" for lovemaking is enhanced.

Various touching-type stimulations—using fingers or a feather or a piece of soft fur—can produce exciting sensations. Try spreading your partner's buttocks, starting some distance away from the anus, and moving slowly, perhaps by a devious path, toward it.

People have said to us, "Oh, I don't think I'd care for any of that. I'm too sensitive there!" Actually such sensitivity (barring a condition requiring medical assistance) may indicate that the person could be especially responsive to anal sensuality if the cultural barriers were lifted.

It is not easy to change attitudes long ingrained by the society one lives in, as a soldier stationed in a southwestern portion of the Mediterranean discovered during World War II. Invited to a banquet at holiday time by a businessman with whom he had become friendly, he was introduced to his host's daughter, a widow with a couple of children. They dated awhile and then went off to her seaside villa for a sexy weekend, with great anticipation. He soon found that what she was anticipating was anal intercourse, the "pleasure" method in her society. She wasn't about to allow vaginal, which was used only for baby making. His protestations that anal contact was perverted were useless. She gradually got over feeling insulted and told him that if they were married she would submit, but only until she got pregnant. Then they could go back to enjoying themselves!

Talk together as freely as possible about your reactions to this chapter thus far. Discuss your possible interest in anal eroticism or your complete disinterest. Remember to use the communication methods that have been outlined. Avoid the "but," the "why," the "because." Don't try to change the other's mind.

Neither partner should initiate anal activity until you've talked about it beforehand and reached an understanding. Talking of itself doesn't necessarily eliminate the taboos, fears, and "protective" responses, but it is a step. The attainment of hearty acceptance of anal activities, *if it should be the couple's desire*, may be spread over weeks, months, or years.

For pleasurable anal stimulation, slowness, gentleness, and ample use of an oil-based lubricant like Vaseline are essential. Approach the anal region with slow, relaxing caresses. As the finger enters, allow sufficient time for the involuntary protective closing actions of the muscles to subside. If your partner makes little clenching movements, you're going too fast. You may not be hurting, but you *are* stirring up fear reactions; *or* you could be hurting. In either case, slow down.

The person who is receiving the lovemaking is to be the monitor and can be aware of any growing apprehension, long before muscle tightening occurs. Communicate! Use the positive approach, such as, "Try going a little more slowly," or, "Wait a minute, and we'll try again." The recipient can help by consciously relaxing the area; opening the anus, as during the bowel movement, promotes easier entrance and heightens pleasurable sensations.

Most people find it difficult to conceive of the anus as an object of admiration and love. After all, "kiss my ass" and "up yours" have been insulting invitations in our society for a long time! Yet we have found that those who have chosen to experience anal sensuality—particularly the women and to some degree the men—recognized a greater love and appreciation of themselves as a result of their partner's loving feelings, so expressed. Having an "ass hole" was something to be happy about. The acceptance of such loving interest is a prerequisite if further exploration and experiences are desired by the couple. The starting point may be only the willingness to experience simple touching and other caressing. Acceptance may come swiftly, it may not come at all. Certainly, *not every couple* is going to be interested.

Take your time with any of the anal activities *if* you decide to try them. A little now, a bit more another time.

Play it by "feel." Recognize that anal love or sensual play usually falls into the category of a special experience. If it doesn't happen to feel right to one or the other, skip it and see what happens another time.

Body positioning for anal intercourse is important. Because the woman should be the monitor of the degree and speed of penetration, in the beginning she should *not* be beneath the man. Anal intercourse becomes more comfortable for the woman as she has more experience; then she may welcome other positions.

Couples frequently assume that anal intercourse automatically means that entry of the penis will be made from the rear, with the woman either kneeling or lying down. Not necessarily! Actually, most positions commonly used in vaginal intercourse will work quite well, each one providing differences in stimulation and response. In the case of one couple who experimented with anal intercourse and liked it, the woman eventually found that the man-on-top position so "ordinary" in vaginal intercourse had extraordinary benefits in anal loving. As she put it, "The weight of his body on me stimulates my clitoris, and *that* sensation gets transferred to my vagina —while his penis is stroking in my anus. Having a response in all three places at once makes for a simply fantastic experience!"

For the uninitiated, the side positions are usually most satisfactory, those in which the husband and wife are both facing in the same direction, spoon fashion or in the Von Urban position (see page 71).

Preliminary relaxation via kissing (lip or deep tongue)

or finger exploration, plus lots of Vaseline are vital. As a measure of the preparation of the woman for penis entry, if her anus can't accept two fingers she isn't ready. The man holds *still*, just guiding his penis with his fingers. The woman actually makes the entry by pushing her anus against it, keeping a firm pressure, while making small circular or sideways movements with her hips, "inviting the penis in," in keeping with her acceptance of penetration. Taking ample time allows pleasurable sensations to dominate. For the neophyte, these feelings may be mixed.

Once entry has been made, the woman decides upon the use of movements that cause penetration and makes them herself. As she becomes more experienced, *if she desires* thrusting movements she can say so, or she can pull the man toward her. Women can enjoy stimulation of the clitoris and the vagina with a finger as an adjunct to anal love.

For the woman, Dorothy says: "There can be three distinct levels of sensation in anal lovemaking. You may not be able to separate them at the start. Things tend to run together, especially if you go too fast.

"The first is around the rim on the outside, or just inside, when your husband is caressing, lightly touching, with his finger or penis. This can be quite stimulating.

"The second, probably the strongest—and *at first* not necessarily the nicest—starts beyond the entrance and gets stronger for an inch or so inside. This is when stretching or "hot" feelings can begin, especially if you're moving too fast or you're not really relaxing enough. The glans will be spreading and expanding this part of you. This is when you must invite the penis in by reaching toward it gently but firmly.

"The third level of feeling comes after the glans has passed that one inch; then there's an abrupt change in sensation. The first one inch is still expanded, but now the feeling and response are different—more sexual. From this point on the penis is really 'in.' Before this, you may both think it is and find, with the attempt to move with rhythm, that it's out. From here on, you can initiate slow, easy, and gentle movements and keep it inside."

Again, we'd like to emphasize that in anal love it is imperative that the *woman* be allowed to initiate the movements that produce deeper penetration by the penis.

A woman who was not in our classes asked for guidance after her first experience. She had felt it was nice at the time, but for the next day or two she had discomfort when having a bowel movement. When questioned about relaxation and lubrication, it became clear they had used none and "plunged right in." No wonder she had problems!

Clearly there should not be any significant pain during or after anal lovemaking. If there is, check the procedure: were you interested and willing, relaxed and ready? Did you use plenty of Vaseline? Was the entry slow?

Keep in mind that some couples may find the penis too large or the anal canal too small for this activity. On the other hand, anal intercourse can produce a level of discomfort, which for some women is overshadowed by pleasurable sensations. "It hurts so good" has been more than one woman's response. That response is quite different from one of *pain!*

A women with a hemorrhoidal condition is not likely to welcome anal intercourse. And yet, a physician who told us that she sometimes used anal dilation as a treatment for patients with this condition, felt that a well-lubricated, gently inserted penis might be equally effective! We offer this view as interesting but without personal recommendation.

People may worry about the presence of bacteria in the anal cavity. What if these get transferred from one place to another? Would this be harmful? Because of the close proximity of the vagina and the anus, free transfer can result, but the vaginal secretions of a healthy woman have natural protective ingredients. This situation ordinarily doesn't present any more of a problem than would the case of a man with poor oral hygiene who might irritate his wife's vagina through oral-genital contact.

For those women who may be prone to disturbances of the vaginal area or of the urethra caused by anal-vaginal transfer, the pitcher douche method should be used whenever going to the toilet. Also, eliminating underpants, or switching to cotton panties (as opposed to nylon), would give greater air contact with the tissues in the area and thus help to retard bacterial activity.

Keep in mind that it isn't necessary to move from the anus to the vagina with the same finger. Keep track of which finger belongs where! Speaking of that, it can be a pleasant experience to have the man gently put a finger in one cavity and the thumb in the other. The tissue between the two cavities is thin, so what goes on in one area, as far as sensation is concerned, can be transferred to the other and vice versa.

Claude observes: "If during anal intercourse the man should move from his wife's anus to her vagina without washing, she *could* have an irritation. However, looking at the situation rationally, we find it hard to imagine a couple in the throes of lovemaking and the man saying, 'Just a minute, darling, I need to go wash my penis!' This may be a hygienically sound idea, but we don't really believe this is the way it happens in real life."

For the man, there is little likelihood of infection as a result of putting his penis into his wife's anus. Some mucous membrane irritation might be possible, but then male homosexuals commonly use anal intercourse, and they seem not to have that problem. If a couple wants anal intercourse but the man fears side effects, he could use a condom. He also could use a condom if either partner is apprehensive about a vaginal transfer and remove it if they should decide to finish in the vagina.

What level of orgasmic response is a woman likely to have with anal love? That depends on the woman. For some, the first few times there may not be much. For others, the first anal contact can produce a rapid and powerful orgasm. One young woman, who at times might have an orgasm with vaginal sex, was persuaded by her lover to try anal intercourse. He was gentle. She had the usual beginner's strong "hot" and "stretching" sensations. As his glans passed the major sphincter, the pleasurable feelings dominated, and she was astonished at how fast and intense was her orgasm.

Another couple were sunbathing in the nude on a remote section of the seashore; the husband fondled his wife's buttocks and anal area in their first experiment with anal caressing. Both wanted to make love, but no condoms were handy, so she suggested they try putting his penis where his fingers had been, to see how that would feel. She was relaxed and ready, so his penis slipped inside with ease. Both experienced a climax. They occasionally made anal love after that, and she became unusually adept. Vaginal stimulation would produce a spontaneous response in her anal region—sphincter relaxation and lubrication—so that if they liked, she could switch his penis from vagina to anus without interrupting their rhythm!

A remarkable transfer of sensations occurred with another woman. She was capable of achieving a mild vaginal orgasm once in a while if everything was "just right." She and her husband heard about anal intercourse and experimented with it, and to her complete delight and surprise she had a "rip-roaring" orgasm like nothing she'd known before. After they had tried this several times she found that the character of her vaginal orgasms became "rip-roaring" too! Perhaps success in itself was a factor; having had a powerful response in one place, she was able to respond vaginally as well.

For most women there is the *opportunity* to have an exciting experience. Pure ecstasy, with an orgasm lasting two or three minutes, was one woman's description.

We have stressed the word "opportunity." There is no guarantee that the experience of every woman will be thrilling. If it is not, she may still have the pleasant feeling of providing her mate with an alternate type of sexual experience. On the other hand, she may be totally uninterested, and that's all right too.

Speaking from the man's view, what's there for him in

penis-anal contact? The anal cavity feels different from the vagina. The little ridgy wrinkles present in the vagina are absent, so the sensations *are* different. Some men report less excitement. You could say that it's like vanilla ice cream *versus* strawberry: both are good, but there's a difference. Because of organ placement, the man may find it easier to contact the cervix with his penis when he's in the anus, even though these are separated by an eighth of an inch of tissue. This can be a very pleasant sensation for both him and his partner.

Some men may experience an extra depth of feeling of oneness with this type of lovemaking: they may sense a profoundly moving "specialness" about it, especially if the woman has an orgasm.

By no means is anal sensual activity the exclusive property of the woman. The male anus is as sensitive as the female's. A wife's fingers, lips, tongue can create remarkable different sensual experiences once the man's hang-ups are set aside—including the vague feeling that interest in anal stimulation may mean he is some sort of repressed homosexual.

One woman wanted to explore her husband's anus with her finger, and, after some discussion, both agreed to try it. She covered the finger with Vaseline, eased it gently inside, slowing down or stopping whenever she felt her husband's anus contracting on her finger. As if she were "seeing" with her finger, she continued exploring. She later reported, with a look of near amazement on her face, how perfectly beautiful her husband felt inside! As a result her attitude toward her husband's body—not only the anal area but his entire structure, and more specifically his genitals—was altered.

Some men may wonder what it feels like to be a woman and be penetrated by a penis. Similarly, a woman may wonder what it's like to *enter* the body of her sexual partner. Exploring this normal curiosity is perfectly all right. The existence of the curiosity may be deeply buried: take a chance and bring it out. As we've said, it's important to discuss such matters, and you don't have to go beyond discussion. If you should decide you *want* to, explore as much or as little as you like.

With the man receiving anal stimulation from his wife, both may share to some degree the experiences of the opposite sex. The woman's lubricated finger inside her husband's anus bears some resemblance to his penis when penetrating her. The male response may be a profound sexual experience of a different nature.

The reversal of roles offers more than sensuality, pleasant though that may be. One young psychologist expressed his opinion that until a man had been "fucked in his ass" (by his wife) he would never become a sensitive lover because he wouldn't appreciate the importance of moving slowly and truly becoming aware of what his partner desired. It also gave him the opportunity to experience the difference between being "cause"—the traditional concept of the male role—and being "effect."

Stimulation of the anal area of the man or the woman with a finger can be delightful spice to regular sexual intercourse. Be sure it's acceptable, be gentle, take your time. Use Vaseline for inside caresses. For the outer rim, saliva will suffice. "Hot" sensations can be all right, but take care that there is no hurting. Finger nails should be smoothed beforehand.

Anal response need not depend upon stimulation by the finger—or, for the woman, by the penis. Some couples stimulate each other with a vibrator, cucumber, etc.; others who are unable or unwilling to welcome a larger object in the anus enjoy the sensations created by a relatively small one (say, a smooth or spiral medium-size birthday candle).

A three-way combination in lovemaking can provide an "overall" experience for the woman. The man penetrates her vagina with his penis, in a side-by-side or kneeling rear-entry position, and then uses clitoral finger stimulation coupled with finger stimulation on the outside of the anus or, if acceptable, inside it.

Anal sensuality, more than any other form of lovemaking, calls for you to sense, to notice the messages from your partner's body, to be aware of each other's movements and body expressions whether it be through simple loving touches, finger exploration, or total anal love.

EXPERIMENTS

1. Affection

Fondle and touch without the intent of climbing right into bed. These can be "love pats" on the genitals, the breasts, etc., caresses that show you really care. Express affection toward the whole person.

Spend some time admiring each other's bodies, including the sexual areas, touching and looking.

2. The Greek Connection

Talk about your feelings and curiosities regarding anal sensuality and your respective "asses," whether these feelings are positive, negative, or neutral. Recall your experiences with toilet training, enemas, suppositories, and so on.

Discuss anal eroticism from your own experiences, if any, and your reactions to this chapter.

If you *both* feel inclined to experiment, OK, but don't force the issue in any way. On the other hand, "don't knock it if you haven't tried it" can apply.

3. For Those Who Are Daring!

If you *both* decide you want to experiment, try this for an introduction.

The woman lies on her side, knees drawn up a bit, and the man lies facing her back.

Apply Vaseline to the anal area.

The woman holds the penis in her hand and strokes the area around the anus and then on the anus with the glans. If need be, for more accessibility, the man can hold up one of her buttocks.

If you want to play "turnabout," the woman faces the man's back and extends a finger, which the man guides with his hand.

4. Love Oil Massage

Recipe: to three ounces of peanut or sesame seed oil, add two teaspoons of peppermint oil, one teaspoon of eucalyptus oil, and one-half teaspoon of either wintergreen, lavender, or clove oil, obtainable from your druggist. If the eucalyptus oil seems too "mediciny," it may be omitted. After mixing, but before using it on the body, put a small amount on a finger and rub it just inside the vagina or just inside the anus. People's sensitivities vary; you must adjust the mixture to your needs. If the sensation is unduly strong, dilute it with peanut or sesame oil. If you don't really feel anything or only slight sensations, increase the amount of the fragrant oils. If you have especially sensitive skin, you must be the judge of whether or not to use the oil.

Gently massage it into the skin from the neck to the toes. Do "both sides." The wife can massage the penis with it. Caution: take care you don't precipitate a premature response! Work the oil around the scrotum. When he's on his belly, spread his buttocks and apply some along the perineum. If your finger happens to find its way into his anus, who knows?, he might like it.

When the man is massaging his partner: anoint her breasts liberally and give tender care to her entire genital area, all the buttons, wrinkles, and folds. If your finger wanders inside her vagina, so much the better. When you turn her over, spread her buttocks and do her anus too, if she desires this.

After anointing, go ahead with your lovemaking. Experience the different feelings generated when your lubricated skins rub together, whether inside or out. Try more than one position, including front to back.

Be aware of each other's movements and body expressions. Check with each other to see if what you are "sensing" is accurate. Notice "messages" from each other's bodies.

11

Variation or Perversion?

Every now and again someone will inquire if our classes in Sexual Repatterning mean we run a swap club. After our emphatic no! the response is sometimes relief—and sometimes disappointment.

The wife-swapping clubs that have burst on the scene in the last dozen years have called forth disbelief, disapproval, and curiosity. The custom of sharing sexual partners is not new: scenes clearly depicting group sexuality form the decorative motif on ancient Grecian bowls and vases, to mention one example. And at the turn of this century, soldiers returning from the Spanish-

American War described partner-swapping parties in Havana which truly ran along "anything goes" lines.

In sections of Germany there is a popular spring ritual that includes wife swapping. *Fasching*, or carnival, lasts a week. Men and women come together for dancing, singing, and other forms of celebration. Marriage partners may elect to go their separate ways and enjoy themselves in whatever manner they wish, which may include sexual contacts. This is considered an opportunity to blow off steam and to relieve bedroom boredom.

Mardi Gras has similar roots, though nowadays the sexual import has been eliminated or toned down. For some couples, however, it still provides an opportunity for sexual exploration outside marriage.

New or not, wife-swapping clubs have stirred enough interest to have books written about them (some serious, some pornographic). According to one report, swap-club members—estimated at five percent of married couples in the United States—have fundamentally sound marriages and believe that they are strengthened by the swapping experience. Other reports characterize swappers as adolescent, immature sensation seekers.

Obviously not all clubs are alike. In some, repeated contacts between two members are encouraged and expected, though everyone must "make the rounds" before a repeat performance. This represents an attempt to avoid extramarital twosome fixations and serves to help maintain a stable membership. Other groups do not permit more than one contact per couple and must expect a large turnover in membership to sustain the clubs.

It is significant that swap clubs of both types have codes of ethics—a "right way"—and established rules.

Basically swappers are seeking variety and freshness in their sexual experiences. We feel that their need for variety in *partners* would vanish if they had variety in sex within their marriages.

Discuss your feelings about swap clubs and the kinds of people who would be attracted to them. We're not suggesting that you join one—only that there is value in sharing and expressing your feelings about everything that is part of the contemporary sexual scene.

As an outgrowth of the swap club, more attention is being focused on the bisexual (or ambisexual) person, one who is equally interested in heterosexual and homosexual loving. In the swap-club context, the bisexual appears as a person for whom a multiplicity of partners of either sex is acceptable, even desirable.

Another addition to the sexual scene is group marriage. Although there have been more instances of failure than success with group-marriage experiments, the idea can be intriguing. One home would serve two families; fewer automobiles might be needed. Were one of the two women oriented toward working outside the home and the other toward homemaking, the needs of each would be met. In the emotional, psychological, and sexual spheres, there would be opportunity for greater variety, according to the agreements made.

As we see it, if there is continuous growth in the relationship of a single couple, and if the couple can develop total sexual response to each other, there would seem to be little advantage to the group approach outside of its economic aspects.

What are your responses to the concept of a group marriage? Do you know anyone who might be in one? Have an open discussion.

Homosexuality is a life style that today is increasingly accepted as a valid sexual preference rather than a perversion. Whether you agree with this or not, it's better to understand and acknowledge homosexuality than to make believe it doesn't exist, as was the case for over a century in most of the Western world. With the more general acceptance of individual preferences today, the homosexual couple no longer need hide their way of life. The true homosexual usually prefers a longer term relationship with someone of the same sex, and some have even expressed the desire to adopt children to round out the family. Sexually, homosexual partners find release and satisfaction doing most of the things heterosexual couples enjoy doing.

Throughout history there has been a place for the female, and sometimes the male, who provides sexual contact for a price. Only rarely does one encounter a culture in which the prostitute is, or was, unknown. Her position in society has ranged from the lowest to the highest—from common streetwalker to cultured courtesan—and in some societies the streetwalker with talent has moved right up through the ranks.

Down through the centuries, the prostitute's basic purpose has remained the same: to provide what her customer could not get at home. In many cases that has meant intercourse, pure and simple. More often, it has meant providing sexual experiences the man has a longing for—things he knows, or believes, his wife would be unwilling to do or things *he* would be unwilling to do with her. Different positions, cunnilingus, fellatio, analingus, anal intercourse—whatever he desires. Again, that variety can be available at home, if he and his wife can develop and share total sexual response.

So far we've been discussing sexual activities that really cannot properly be called "variants." But what of human-animal sexual contacts? We have been taught to view these with revulsion or abhorrence, despite the fact that mythology and history offer plenty of references to sexual contacts between man and animals (or rather, mankind and animals, for the human female has participated as well as the male).

In today's society, animal-human sexual contacts still occur, most frequently in rural areas where both the animal and the privacy are readily available. Goats, sows, calves, ewes, and mares have been used by boys and young men, and not just in novels! In the city, there are household animals. The manner in which cats and dogs communicate by licking has been a source of erotic stimulation for children and some adults. The kitten playing beneath the bedclothes with her young mistress can be induced, with relative privacy, to lick the labia, the clitoris, or the anal area. (The roughness of a cat's tongue may produce rather mixed sensations; a dog or puppy's tongue, being smoother, produces a lighter level of sensation.)

Less common is the type of sensual experience that happened while one couple was sunbathing nude in a secluded area. They had been sipping away on a bottle of wine and fondling each other; the woman had her knees spread wide apart and was enjoying the warmth of the sunshine between her thighs. Presently a wandering insect alighted on her labia. Feeling relaxed, she didn't immediately shoo it away. The minute, concentrated stimulation created by the insect as it moved delicately over vulva and clitoris was not so much sexual as intensely sensual. While not often recorded, references to this type of experience do exist.

Classical psychology has some harsh-sounding names for practices that are, in our opinion, harmless sexual variations. We recall a man who would ask his wife to leave him a pair of her unlaundered panties when she was to be away from home for a few days. He liked to smell her smell, a form of comfort in her absence. Is this fetishism? Maybe. What do you think?

One woman liked to bring her husband to orgasm by sliding his penis in between her ample breasts; she then used his semen as a body lotion. Is that a perversion? We don't think so, any more than we think the woman who likes to nurse on her husband's penis or the man who feels that way about his wife's labia or clitoris are perverted. We know a husband who sometimes wears his wife's jewelry; they both enjoy, in private, "decorating him"!

If both partners like now and then to spank or be spanked (lightly), switch or be switched, fine! We don't get turned on by that, but if *they* do. . . . If a woman gets a thrill from being tied to the bed, and it arouses her partner too, well, have fun, we say. The main thing is the mutual desire and agreement.

The use of foods on or in the woman's genitals is neither new nor perverted. For the special delight of her customer, the Roman courtesan used honey. As a prelude for other pleasures to come, her client would lick and suck the honey away, enjoying, simultaneously, two different types of oral gratification. (Meanwhile, it is quoted, "She could writhe in all manner of lusty responses.") Today, couples have been known to try everything from whipped cream to caviar, yogurt to peanut butter, mashed banana to sauces or jams. There's no need to confine such garnishing to the woman; the man's apparatus can be just as much fun.

A few years ago, when peppermint-flavored toothpaste became popular, a man who had just brushed his teeth and still had a residue of toothpaste in his mouth performed cunnilingus on his partner. The two of them discovered what "hot" sensations a little toothpaste can produce. (That same couple may have experimented with a dab on his penis, thereby inventing mint-flavored intercourse!) If you want to try this, use only a *small* amount.

The upturned vagina is said to have been used as a wine goblet in the revelings of Bacchus, the ancient god of wine. We see no reason why amorous modern-day wine drinkers need deny themselves the delights of such an exotic goblet. The woman can lie on her back, legs drawn up to her chest, hips elevated as needed. Any wine you both like will do, but we might mention that champagne is said to produce a special sensation. If you're not a wine drinker, you might consider beer or ginger ale.

Some couples we teach have expressed curiosity about various "sex aids" used routinely in Oriental countries and now available here. They include aids to masturbation as well as items to be used together by a couple. If you too are curious, you might check the advertisements in an "adult magazine." Be prepared for a flood of material if you answer one ad!

One woman came to us in some consternation after she found a cache of pornographic pictures and novels while cleaning out her husband's closet. Was she failing him sexually? Or was he perverted? We asked if she'd looked at the material; she admitted that she had and that "some of the pictures were pretty exciting." We recommended that she suggest looking at the material *with* her husband. She did and later said that he responded most enthusiastically to this shared experience. At last report, they had had a fine time attending a blue movie together.

Now and again we encounter students who hesitantly mention their pleasure in the warm feeling of their partner's urine. (Fresh urine, from a healthy person, is virtually sterile. It has been used on the battlefield to cleanse wounds when clean water was not available.) One man would sometimes say to his wife during intercourse, "Honey, pee a little and make it feel better!" His wife enjoyed the sensations too. They wondered if this was a perversion. We think not, so long as they both enjoyed the activity.

On the other hand, a woman was granted a divorce because she was offended by her husband's *insistence* that, each time they had intercourse, he urinate inside her at the close. Clearly this was not mutually acceptable.

• 151

The anal area, so rich in nerves, can be erotically stimulated by an enema. One woman told us that she and her husband would give each other an enema as a sensual experience. We suspect that this is a more common practice than is ordinarily assumed.

Even though both parties agree to the sexual activities we've discussed, some states and municipalities have statutes forbidding some of them. A few years ago, *Time* magazine reported the plight of a man in one of the New England states. He and his wife both enjoyed anal intercourse now and then. In a blaze of anger after a quarrel, she reported an anal contact to the police. When she "cooled down" she tried to retract her statement, but the court found him guilty and sentenced him to ten years. Eventually the American Civil Liberties Union took his case to a higher court, which decided that what a consenting married couple do in the privacy of their bedroom is of no concern to the state.

Where couples want sexual activity that is prohibited by law, they may have felt inhibited. With more sensible rulings being issued, they may feel freer to conduct their lives as they wish and to make their own decisions as to what may be satisfying, novel, refreshing, or revitalizing to their love life. Together they can give themselves permission to do what *they* choose in bed. What's proper or improper becomes a matter of agreement.

How is one to decide which is which? We think the answer lies in knowledge, in freedom from preconceived notions, and in one's own personal preferences framed within the concept of *appropriateness*.

152 ·

What sexual activities *are* perverted? you may wonder, if the activities we've discussed thus far do not, in our opinion, fit that category—however they may be categorized by our puritanical society. As we see it, any activity conducted in an appropriate setting and mutually acceptable to two sexual partners that *does not harm either of them* is OK and not a perversion. The activities chosen may not be widely enjoyed, but by the same token not every couple likes escargots, scuba diving, or Monopoly.

What *do* we consider perversions? Unprovoked, forcible rape is an obvious perversion, as is the attaining of sexual pleasure through suffering, mutilation, or death. (Here is one example that qualifies, we think: in a prewar Parisian brothel, the anal cavity of a turkey was made available for the client's penis. At the moment of climax, an attendant would wring the bird's neck so that its dying spasms produced muscular contractions to heighten the man's sensations.)

We consider perversion to be an attitude of disregarding or ignoring the expressed feelings and distress of another. It is the subjugation or degradation of an individual against his or her will for the sake of the aggressor's "pleasure" that is perverted. The aggressor is, indeed, treating a fellow human as a "thing."

Ultimately, perversion is monitored by individual and group beliefs and differs from time to time and place to place. Each one of us might well draw a different line between the natural and the perverse. Variation is by no means necessarily perversion!

EXPERIMENTS

1. First, Let's Talk

Discuss this chapter together. What kinds of sexual activity have you assumed to be perverted? Have you felt that unusual sexual activities were "sick"? Which ones? Talk together about any "unusual" experiences you may have had or imagined having.

2. A Loaf of Bread, a Jug of Wine—and Thou!

Have a very special meal in a secluded room—your bedroom would be fine. Sit on the floor, on pillows, and naturally in the nude.

The meal is to consist of a variety of finger foods: small amounts of ten or twelve different things to be dipped in sauces, spread on crackers, and so on. Decide together which ones you'd like to have; shop for them and prepare them together.

Select a variety of flavors as well as textures: sweet, salty, bitter or sour; smooth, crunchy, chewy, stringy. Vary the liquids you serve with the meal, too—juices, wine, etc. Use your imagination.

Now, feed each other one bite at a time, taking turns. Be aware of your senses: smell, taste, and touch (within the mouth). Before you take the food in your mouth, be sure to smell its odors. That applies not only to the bite you are receiving but to any residual odors on your partner's fingers.

3. Try a New One

Choose an "unusual" sexual activity or position you've never tried before, one that appeals to both of you. Stay with it for a while, if not all the way.

4. The "Glowing" Candle

The woman is to massage love oil (see experiment in the preceding chapter) into the opening at the tip of her partner's penis. Use enough to create a nice "glow." Carry on with your own choice from there.

5. Music Hath Charms

Make love to music. Tune in to the "mood" of the selection. Pretend you are dancing; move your bodies as you would if you *were* dancing.

6. The Artist's Colony

Buy water-base colors and experiment with body painting. The results can be interesting, erotic, amusing, or downright hilarious. For a start, nipples can be painted as eyes—you take it from there. If you have a Polaroid camera, you might enjoy taking pictures of your efforts.

7. Ice Power

The woman takes an ice cube in her mouth and then adds the penis. The sensations for the man become quite intense (the procedure, in fact, is reputed to guarantee an erection when nothing else will do the job). The woman can also slip an ice cube into her vagina (once you get it past the opening it feels all right) and then proceed with intercourse. True, the ice will melt and drip, but the sensation can make a little mess worthwhile!

12

Aphrodisiacs and Love Potions

Like many things that have to do with sexuality in our culture, information on aphrodisiacs and love potions—when available at all—has been garbled and contradictory. Aphrodisiacs have been held, variously, to be "all in the mind," evocative of sensual feelings, or productive of urgent sexual desire or engorgement of the genitals.

Some substances that weaken the barriers to response by reducing inhibitions and stimulating fantasy have been mislabeled as aphrodisiacs. And over a thousand foods, including quite ordinary items, have at some time or other been said to be sexual stimulants—from artichokes to yeast, bird's-nest soup to a sow's vulva!

Reports of the aphrodisiacal qualities of marijuana are contradictory. Many smokers attest that a mild high enhances sex in various ways; other evidence suggests that, far from being a sexual stimulant, marijuana can operate in the opposite fashion.

Accurate data on the sexual effects of mescaline and LSD are meager. These hallucinogenic drugs possibly heighten sexual interest by reducing inhibitions or by evoking erotic hallucinations.

Damiana, in the form of a liquor made from the dried leaves of a Mexican shrub, is said to produce local stimulation and engorgement of the sex organs when used in sufficient quantity—whatever that may be, since reliable information is difficult to come by. As an herb tea, it is available in some stores. We have found from personal experience that there can be some slight tendency toward urethral irritation in the modest quantities usually taken: one cup of the herb tea made according to the directions on the box.

In Oriental lore, ginseng, the peculiarly shaped root plant that looks like a divided carrot, is said to have strong stimulative powers. Personally, we like it as a tea. In our experience, it *might* have some sexual stimulative effect—that is, "If you think it does, it probably will."

There is another class of stimulants said to have aphrodisiac qualities. As Ogden Nash put it, "Candy is dandy, but liquor is quicker." In the strict sense of the word, alcohol is *not* an aphrodisiac. As with the psychedelic-type drugs, alcohol works by releasing the inhibitions. Regardless of how it functions, in the proper dosage it can encourage an abandoned lovemaking session for those so inclined. Too much is a real "bummer" for sex. At best, inebriation reduces sexual sensations; at worst, it makes erection for the man and orgasm for both partners difficult or impossible.

Champagne, for some people, has long enjoyed a reputation for being an elegant source of sexual titillation. Frankly, we agree with this viewpoint. On special occasions we like the idea of a brunch *preceded* by an appropriate amount of champagne. Between the champagne and the brunch, we sandwich delectable, floaty sex.

On the other hand, we know couples who, after two glasses of champagne, are ready for bed but not for sex! Knowing and understanding your personal responses to so-called stimulants is important. And keep in mind the fact that dependence on artificial stimulation results in an eventual decrease of *natural* sensual and sexual feelings. Why is this so? Because the responsibility for one's state of being and doing is assigned outside of the self: " '*It*' makes me feel that way."

We know that a healthy, well-balanced diet with optimal amounts of vitamins and minerals can do much more toward stimulating sexual vigor. That statement is equally true said in reverse: a diet that is deficient in nutritional factors and vitamins will almost invariably cause a diminution of sexual vigor.

That's all very well, you may feel, but what about the "obvious" aphrodisiacs? Could they "liberate" me? How might I behave?

Looking at some of these substances, we can see that they may free a person from self-imposed restrictions or encourage sexual fantasy. Others may generate genital irritation, which masquerades as *sexual intent*.

Certainly a person whose inhibitions are down can more easily move into expression of a pseudosexy feeling. There should, however, be a detectable difference between genital irritation and genuine sexual arousal in a man or woman. For example, cantharides ("Spanish Fly") doesn't make a woman "hot;" it makes her *itch* inside her vagina!

The real question is whether or not one can turn on the sexual power of fantasy, release inhibitions, and reach a high level of awareness *without* drugs or aphrodisiacs or artificial stimulants of any kind. We believe that "turn on" to be eminently possible.

The key is fantasy.

Before you begin to explore fantasy in the following chapter, we suggest that you try these five experiments, designed to sharpen your perceptions and self-awareness. You might think of them as ways to expand your consciousness, to "turn on," without drugs.

EXPERIMENTS

1. Hearing Your World

Close your eyes, and listen to the sounds in and out of the room. Really *listen*. Pick up the distant sounds of an automobile, a train, a bird. Listen for any creaking in the bed or chair.

If the room is very quiet, you may be able to hear the sounds of your own body functioning. Put your hands over your ears and listen. Share what you find.

For a combined hearing and touching experience, turn on a radio or record player quite loud and then place your hands on the speaker. *Feel* the sound as well as hearing it. If practical, sit on the speaker cabinet, and feel the sounds with your buttocks and genital area. A selection featuring lots of thumpy drums or a plucked bass is good for this experiment.

2. Seeing May Indeed Be Believing

In this experiment, you will be asked to project a definite feeling as you say certain words. Watch for changes in your partner's body attitudes, facial responses, movements, projected feelings. Be aware of your own responses and emotions.

Sit cross-legged in the nude, on floor or bed, facing

each other and fairly close together. If either of you wears eyeglasses, leave them off.

Whoever goes first should say to the other, "You may look at me," and project that feeling. The partner looks. After a moment, say (and project the feeling), "You may not look at me." The partner continues to look anyway. Now switch to, "You may look into me"; then, "You may not look into me." Finish with, "You may look at me."

Share your responses to the various word patterns, the feelings you sensed within yourself and your partner. Were any of these feelings familiar? Did you discover anything new?

After you have shared as much as possible, switch roles.

3. Awareness through Touch

Whoever goes first: have your partner lie down nude on the bed, couch, or floor.

Close your eyes, and explore the nude body from head to toe with your finger tips. The intent is not to stimulate sexual response but to "see" his or her body through your finger tips. If you like, ask your partner to turn over or turn on one side or move a body part.

The person being touched is to be *aware* of being "seen" by the finger tips.

Both of you are to experience and share feelings, attitudes, new discoveries, responses, pleasure, displeasure, enjoyment, boredom—whatever may arise.

Now exchange roles.

4. Cuddling

Holding each other, cuddle and fondle, but do not let the cuddling progress to lovemaking.

Be relaxed in your positions. Do as much stroking as you like, but for at least part of the time just lie close together, quietly.

5. Turn About

When you are going to make love, agree that the woman will place all her attention inside her vagina and the man on his penis. Then exchange, with the man focusing into the vagina and the woman on the penis.

Continue alternating the focus. After the lovemaking, share your experiences.

On another occasion, repeat the experiment and imagine that you are: first, your own vagina or penis; second, your partner's vagina or penis. Compare experiences.

At other times, do the experiment without telling your partner until afterward.

13

Sharing Sexual Fantasies

The art of fantasy, as we refer to it here, involves returning to the imaginative viewpoints of childhood. The key is the willingness to share, with your partner, even those fantasies that may be uncomfortable to admit.

Begin the process by bringing out of hiding and sharing little "safe" fantasies with each other. As you listen, project an accepting attitude toward your partner. Gradually, you will find it easier to talk about fantasies you once considered taboo.

People tend to assume that they have to live out their fantasies once they are discussed. Certainly one *can*

164 •

transform fantasy into reality—that's the essence of invention, of creativity—but there is no *requirement* that this be done. In fact, talking about fantasies without necessarily acting them out is a way of becoming acquainted with a previously hidden part of yourself.

Such sharing can produce freedom from tension or anxiety. This proved to be the case for a small-breasted woman who felt angry and anxious whenever her husband glanced at a well-endowed woman. Her fantasies about what his thoughts and wishes might be would make her miserable. After this couple became adept in their fantasy sharing, the husband felt he could openly look at another woman's breasts—together, they could talk about how big they were. The wife *knew* what he was thinking and did not have to torture herself with her fantasies.

When you share experiences, you usually find "secret corners" where you have tucked away interests and curiosities about a lot of things other than sexuality. Sharing these provides a wealth of opportunities to explore. There are fantasies worthy only of being "dumped"; others may be worth testing against reality. Some you may laugh about; others may contain real concerns.

Dorothy gives an example. "Claude and I had our separate fantasies about having a totally satiating weekend, to be spent in bed, making love! After sharing the fantasy, we decided to make it come true. Off we went to a remote mountain cabin for complete privacy. We were really enjoying ourselves when a knock on the door interrupted us. It seems the cabin was for sale, and the real-estate man wanted to show the place. We dressed, cleared away the signs of our orgy, and retreated to the porch. When the people drove off, I asked Claude if he'd like to resume. Doubtless influenced by his by then soft penis, he said he'd like to sit on the porch and admire the view for a while.

"Presently we were hungry, so we ate, and then back to bed we went. Not too long after that, I began to feel tired of lying down. This was only one day into our fantasy, and reality—the real-estate agent, the limp penis, hunger, not to mention fatigue—was taking over.

"We sat around and talked until two A.M., so we slept late the next day. And what was the first thing we thought about? *Food!* Then back to bed. Before noon we began to run out of things to do.

"We backed away and shared our views, which turned out to be the same for each of us—'I've had enough, I'm tired of fucking!'

"Our conclusion? It's impossible—for us, anyway—to spend all weekend just making love. That happens only in novels."

We are convinced couples need to acknowledge when "they've had it," *whatever* the activity. Listen to the inner voice, realize when reality and wishes don't match. This can be hindsight, and that's OK. When it's time to "let go," do so with no regrets.

Regrets can become the fodder for wishful thinking: "If only I'd. . . ." Fantasy sharing is a safe way to examine the leftovers of wishful thinking, to determine how much risk one is willing to take. Taking a risk means being responsible in the real world, making decisions and carrying out actions that initiate the excitement of a new experience.

An important aspect of marriage is the continuing excitement in the total relationship. Besides the variations in sexual activities we have discussed, some games and acting out may be refreshing.

One couple with a theatrical background liked to arrange a change of scene for themselves. The wife, wearing clothes different from her normal attire, a wig, and makeup appropriate to the change, would go and sit at a bar; her husband would drop in and pick her up. They would have dinner, go to a hotel and make love, and then separate to return home individually. They might continue the game by alluding to the date with a "stranger." They felt it was a great spice for their marriage.

Setting things up so the man can rip off an old nightgown or dress can be a source of excitement. Some couples really enjoy, now and then, playing rape, with emphasis here on *playing*. Or there can be the excitement of playing "hard to get" (assuming each of you knows it is play).

Games, if enjoyable to both, are additional ways of "taking risks," experimenting with new feelings in the bedroom relationship. Seek ways to find something surprising, something new, to experience together. Do this in your everyday living too. Break up the old routines: eat meals at different times from your usual schedule; trade sides of the bed. If the two of you are alone for a weekend, try getting along without clocks or watches, living your life as you sense it. Eat, sleep, and get up when you feel ready, whatever the hour.

Most of us have been reared on the fantasy of "romantic love." Nourished by books and movies, "love" has been considered *the* important aspect of marriage. We think this can lead to the sad situation where a couple may love each other without liking each other—and liking each other, in our view, is more essential to a good marriage. Its presence provides an honest base for the development of loving feelings.

In the "romantic love" fantasy, the loved one meets every unspoken need, knows exactly how the other feels and thinks. In a real marriage, what this boils down to could be dependency upon fantasy instead of communication. It is unrealistic to expect all-knowingness in a mate. In the sexual area particularly, the expectation that he or she should know what you want and provide it without being asked is unreasonable, to say the least. The attitude stems in part from the secrecy surrounding sexual activity during childhood, in part from what is left in us as the result of the instant gratification of our needs in infancy. It is a mystique so deeply rooted that when we suggest to couples that they talk together about what things they would like to have the other do to them or with them or for them, we are met almost with indignation.

"If I have to ask for something," they say, "it spoils the fun."

Certainly there can be pleasure in being surprised

when your partner does precisely the thing you want done when you want it. But after all, at the present stage of mankind's development, ESP is the rarity rather than the rule. Consider how many possible variations of sexual activity, ranging from the prelude to the postlude, we have mentioned thus far, and you begin to realize how unusual it is for your partner to hit upon the special one desired at the precise time.

When neither of you tells the other what you enjoy most, the possibilities of satisfaction will be remote indeed. We think it is important that you talk together about the types of sexual activity you like, those you have not used as often along with those you have, and even those you have never tried but that may seem intriguing. Then it may be possible for you to "expect" things without being disappointed.

There will be little benefit in such discussion unless each partner understands the other's wishes, remembers what they are, and, most important, does something about them.

If one or the other doesn't remember often enough, provide reminders pleasantly, without accusatory tones. The approach could be "I think it would be fun to do so-and-so," or "I'm ready for such-and-such." The partner's response, hopefully, will be to fulfill the desire as speedily as is practical *or* discuss any objections. The failure to do so, or to communicate within an appropriate time span, can damage the quality of your life together, sexual and otherwise.

EXPERIMENTS

1. Did You Ever Think of Trying——?

Delve into your mind for those funny little things you thought about doing but never did. Bring them out, dust them off, and talk about them. Maybe you won't want to do them; maybe you will. Either way is all right.

One man confessed his fantasy of sucking on his wife's clitoris while his penis was in her vagina—impossible, but they had fun sharing the idea.

2. Two-Track Stereo

While making love, share aloud your feelings and sensations as you go along.

3. Fantasizing with Your Senses

In fantasy: be aware of your favorite smell, then of a happy smell, an animal smell, a flower smell, an outdoor smell, a sexy smell. Share with each other what you are experiencing.

With your eyes closed, be aware of your favorite color. (If you don't have a favorite color, pick one for the moment.) See your favorite color as a part of some object. Now choose several other colors in turn and do the same. Share your experiences.

In your fantasy, hear the sound of music, any music; hear a happy sound, an animal sound, an outdoor sound, a sexy sound. Share your experiences.

4. A Funny Thing Happened on the Way . . .

As optional experiments, from time to time, if *both agree*, act out:

Slave girl and sultan; prostitute and customer (either way!); empress and consort; ripping off an old dress or nightgown; a rape scene; a virgin (either way!); hard to get (either way!); two strangers. (This last one can be revealing. Pretend you don't know the other's body, likes, dislikes, and so on.)

14

No Older Than You Think

The ancients made provision for phases of growth and development in the life cycle. Each time a person moved into a new stage of life—a new level of responsibility or self-expression—it was an occasion for ritual, celebration, initiation. The end as well as the beginning of a stage was appropriately noted.

Our culture pays scant attention to the stages in the life cycle. The American male is more likely to "observe" his wife's menopause by having an affair! We offer each other little recognition of the inner needs that emerge as we move from one phase to the next. And yet, if the marriage relationship has grown in depth through the years, the transfer of impulsive, youthful ardor to a full, totally satisfying sexual understanding in later years, when children are grown and gone, can be done smoothly. The sexual fires may then burn with a less frequent yet warmer glow.

When that transition does not occur, divorce has become the all-too-prevalent solution. With the slowing of passion in the forties and fifties, marriages are shipwrecked: the absence of warmly fulfilling attitudes toward each other, coupled with the bedroom slowdown, has left no base for the relationship. Where the flow of sexual energy from one partner to the other has been accepted, even augmented through conscious effort, the banking of passion and diminished urgency for orgasm need *not* diminish fulfillment. The communication of man and woman in a loving relationship, with or without climax, can be wonderfully satisfying.

Recognition and willingness to participate in each other's flow of sexual energy does not appear miraculously at some fortuitous moment. Like the total response we have discussed, it is to be practiced, experienced, and valued as a part of your sexual growth and maturing. In so doing, you prepare the way for future fulfillment.

When it comes to sexual frequency, what is "normal"—as with other aspects of sexuality—is in fact highly individual. What would be scarcity for one couple is abundance for another. There are couples in their twenties who find sex once or twice a month satisfying, and people in their eighties who have it twice a day! Looking for the norms can be a covert way of justifying a belief that you're not getting enough, or too much. Couples should realize that usually, *but by no means always*, frequency declines with the passage of the years. What is appropriate at one time may not be appropriate at another for the same couple. Change is a natural function of all living beings; it should be welcomed, explored, and accepted as such.

As a man and woman, older or younger, move toward making their sexual communion more fulfilling, their frequency pattern *may* change. If this happens, it should in no way be considered a cause for concern or apprehension. In cultures where couples are taught before marriage how to achieve a full level of response, one sexual contact in five to seven days has been found to be satisfying. That statement is *not* intended as a recipe! Find your own way, together.

Skin-to-skin contact, being held or stroked by one's mate, is a powerful and legitimate human need. Some women entice men, not because they want intercourse but because they want to be cuddled. The "price" they pay is sex! Some women report that they find being held more satisfying than sexual contact; even prostitutes have admitted that being held by the male customer often fulfills a deep wish. In the average human being, both longings can blend together, or each can be present at different times. The point is: they can be (and it is good for them to be) two separate activities that *may* but *need not be* blended.

The two of us do a lot of cuddling, both in and out of bed. Sometimes it leads to sexual contact; more often it does not. Dorothy has a deep-down need for it. As a premature baby, she had *no* holding from anyone until she was six weeks old. She describes her feelings about this as "a mixture of rejection, aloneness, self-pity, and 'what's wrong,' laced with frustration." She says: "Part of me *very early* accepted a role of 'do it for yourself—take care of yourself.' Without self-growth and understanding, I could easily have allowed my deep hunger and yearning for physical closeness to go underground to be lived out in unhealthy ways."

If you think the wish to be held is "childish," consider that thought a hang-up you could do without! Men have this need as well as women, but it's more difficult for them to express it. Talk about it together. Maybe he'd like some too if he could feel OK about accepting.

Your marriage bed is the superhighway to the satisfaction of so-called childish desires. We believe that parts of ourselves didn't get enough holding and touching from our parents. When our needs can be fulfilled by our mate, that helps to round out our growth—which includes the ability to give *and* receive affection.

The menopause can be a time when the woman has mixed feelings toward the receiving and the giving of affection. Hormonal changes are taking place that can cause pain and discomfort during intercourse, but these and other physical symptoms can be relieved medically. *Emotional* symptoms—fluctuations in mood and responsiveness, feeling no longer desirable or "sexy"—benefit most from understanding on the part of husband *and* wife.

For the woman, the menopause represents the end of

one facet of feminine sexuality: reproduction. By no means does it represent the end to her sexual responsiveness unless she decides it shall be that way. If she is looking for a good excuse to reject her sexuality, the "trials" of the menopausal period can be used as the opportunity to close the door, and the man will look elsewhere for sex. For the woman who accepts her mature sexuality, the menopause may be a blessing, an opportunity for her to enjoy lovemaking wholeheartedly—without fear of pregancy or use of contraceptives.

Though less generally recognized, the man also reaches a time of hormonal rebalancing. For the couple who have developed a feeling of closeness with meaningful, varied, and fulfilling sexual response, the onset of the man's climacteric period can be an opportunity for new experiences together. The woman who expresses and offers her understanding, encouragement, and reassurance, will help the man deal with the anxiety generated by the diminishing of frequency and vigor of erection. Quips about "being over the hill" are out of place. To the frightened male, this is not a joking matter.

In America and Western Europe a premium is placed on the "vertical penis." Other societies accept the fact that gratifying sex is possible with the penis not fully erect. The woman simply lubricates her vagina to receive it.

A satisfactory entry may be made with a slack penis if the side or "spoon" position is used: the woman "sits on the man's lap" while they both lie on their sides. Some couples may prefer the Von Urban position (see page 83). The head of the penis needs to be guided into the parted lips. Sometimes the sensation of this entry may generate a "half-mast erection," or movements afterward may do so. Whether or not the semierection materializes is unimportant. The goal is the opportunity to sense the warmth, the flow of feeling, that can develop when this type of contact is maintained for twenty-five to thirty minutes. And, the "opening up" that a woman can offer her partner in bed during this period can spill over into other, nonsexual aspects of their lives.

For the couple who have had a *one-sided* sexual life, the beginning of hormonal changes in either may spell the end of sex activity. As the drive toward frequent sex diminishes, the lessened urge is likely to be overpowered by the partner's resistance. The couple may just tend to give sex up as "too much trouble": when the body isn't clamoring so loudly, it may seem simpler to let the whole thing slide. With the diminution of sexual activity, the speed of the aging process—of body functioning as well as mental efficiency—may be stepped up. Healthy, hearty sexual expression is, on the other hand, an excellent means of staying more youthful, more vigorous, more vital.

EXPERIMENTS

1. What's in Store for Us?

Discuss together all the old wives' tales you can recall about menopause *and* the man's climacteric. ("You lose all sex feelings." "That's the end." "Some women lose their minds." "Men grow impotent.") Include what your parents or relatives told you or complained about.

Together, examine your attitudes to both. Are you "supposed" to behave a certain way during menopause? Do you have "scary" feelings about it? What does the man feel?

2. Heightened Skin Awareness

During this experiment share what each of you is experiencing at the time or afterward.

Lie on your sides, face to face, with as much skin contact as possible. Reach out mentally with your awareness. Be aware of the skin on your own back, the surface that is away from the partner. Allow five minutes or so to become as aware as you can of all sensations, imagery, attitudes, and feelings. These may change as you go along.

Transfer awareness to the surface that is in contact with the other person, and repeat.

Be aware of the space *between* your two skins. Take five or ten minutes for experiencing the sensations.

On another occasion, repeat the experience with the woman lying on her side facing away from the man and the man facing the woman's back; or with the man facing forward, the woman facing his back; or try man on top, then woman on top.

3. Butterfly Massage

The person who goes first lies quietly, nude, in a candle-lit room.

The other person, *very lightly* and *very slowly*, moves the finger tips over the body of the receiver. Begin away from erogenous zones, then move toward them gradually. The finger pads should *barely* touch the skin (or hair).

The receiver is to focus attention on the sensations and allow sexual ones to build (if they do) as well as sensual ones.

Communicate what is being experienced.

Exchange roles and repeat.

4. Sharing Fantasies for Fun

Using the fantasy sharing in the preceding chapter as a model, continue to share whatever fantasies turn up—now and in the future. Use no criticism or censure, make no attempt to "change" fantasies that your partner may have. Most of us have fun enough with our fantasies so that we don't need encouragement from the partner, although appreciation might be expressed where appropriate.

5. Fantasies about or with Each Other

Make up a sexual fantasy about your partner, initially keeping it to yourself. Include the feelings, the body movements, the sounds, the facial and other gestures, the climax, and the aftermath. When you've finished creating your fantasy, share it with your mate.

6. Now I Lay Me Down

When you are ready for sleep, find a comfortable position in which each of you can place a hand, palm down, on the other's genitals.

As you fall asleep, be aware of what you are sensing—both in your own and in your partner's hand and genitals.

15

The Miracle of Sexual Energy

In marriage, the importance of liking each other and freely showing warmth and affection cannot be stressed enough. If you feel that you cannot yet make a distinction between simple physical affection and sexual desire, explore the situation together. Examine the possibilities of projecting warmth between you, allowing it to remain just that.

We see the projection of warm feelings, toward anyone, as a form of transmission of "energy." We have chosen the term *energy*, although it is a misnomer, to describe that "something" which may be sensed between two people. This cannot be measured by any instrument, and there isn't even a good word in the language to express it.

The exchange of sexual energy between mates can't be measured either, but some people, especially those who have freed themselves from inhibitions and respond fully, experience it. "When we began to sense this," Claude explains, "we started comparing and discussing our experiences. Tentatively we accepted the possibility of an energy flow, and we explored our sensory impressions toward one another."

"As we went along, finding our own way," Dorothy continues, "we began to open ourselves to new sensory awareness. This was the beginning of some rather exciting and unusual extrasensory experiences. We clearly felt sexuality to be a pathway toward greater self-awareness, a springboard to spiritual growth and development. In the beginning we felt this concept was a bit 'kooky.' But as we explored other cultures, we found we weren't the first to emerge with this idea, not by any means."

In the teachings of an Indonesian mystic, the woman is said to be the more powerful transmitter of energy during a sexual contact, sending strong levels to the body of the man. These levels, it is said, may or may not be consciously detected by the male, depending upon his level of sensitivity. If the feelings of the woman are negative, angry, resentful, resistive, they can set up negative responses of a related nature in the man. If the emanations from the woman are positive—warm, loving, appreciative—the man's response has a matching quality.

"Strange though this may seem," Dorothy observes,

"it does have a significant place in the man-woman relationships. If a woman is mated to a sensitive man, there is no use kidding herself. She can't fool him about how she feels. Better to be honest!

"The old concept of a woman doing her duty regardless is just out. Those feelings of hers are going into the man's body. Claude says that he can sense 'feeling' transmission not only through his penis, but also in the region around his genital area. He *knows* when my feelings are in opposition to what I'm saying or doing."

"Between us," Claude says, "there are warm and wonderful feelings when we make love. If we feel disagreeable toward each other, we don't attempt to take it out on each other in bed. We believe in clearing away any negative feelings *before* coming together for lovemaking."

When two people have allowed their ideas about sexuality and marriage to merge and emerge, when they feel a "consummate closeness," *then* may come the time when the energy transfer is strong enough to make the body glow or generate color. We feel this experience to be an outward symbol of spiritual maturing through sexuality.

Dorothy explains: "I experience it as either a bluish white or yellowish white that emanates from Claude's body. I find this hard to describe. It is as if the light consists of many threads going out and away from him for a distance and then disappearing. I know it is coming from him because if I place my hand between my eyes and his body I can see where my hand is blocking the glow. When I press on his skin and then take it away, the light flares up stronger in that space. This glowing often happens when we have had a warm sexual communion. I sense that the glow is more frequent than I am able to perceive, and as my awareness continues to expand, I hope to 'see' the 'life force,' as I think of it, more clearly and more often."

Claude says: "Although I don't see a glow from Dorothy's body, I do have visions of strong energy flows that seem to be passing between our bodies. I feel these flows within my body too, and for me they have color. I see blue or purple and sometimes a faint gold—whether my eyes are open or closed. Sometimes I see points of golden light around the room, but these are generated in my head because if I move my head they don't move on the visual field."

Dorothy says: "When Claude has one of these color experiences the energy flow from his body is very strong. In the beginning of our relationship, this made me uncomfortable. I felt overwhelmed. As I came to understand what was happening, I began to feel as if I were having a warm bath."

Sexuality encompasses dimensions beyond the sensate expression. Released sexuality provides an ambiance for profound psychological and spiritual growth. We view it as a good pathway to experiencing altered states of consciousness *without* the use of drugs.

Love, we feel, is the integration of two energy streams, male and female, brought about by the sacramental union. With this blending, a third "something" is created, like the green that appears when blue and yellow merge. It is our conviction that through warm, ever-growing sexual-spiritual communion we have, all our lives, the means to increase the store of energy available to us.

Marriage, we believe, offers the ideal setting for this experience. Research (Dr. Kegel's and others') has shown that contact with a multiplicity of partners works *against* the goal of a fine-tuned sexual harmony. The kind of communication we have been discussing does not emerge from short-term relationships; a man or woman with a variety of sexual partners is not at all likely to achieve complete satisfaction, to come to this kind of sexual maturity.

To experience a balance of sexual, sensual, and emotional responses, a total loving relationship is essential —and this means in day-to-day living. The fruits of loving inspiration can be denied to the promiscuous. It is as simple as that.

We are advocates of variety with one's own partner—from a purely practical standpoint, not a religio-moralistic one. Both of you, together, can free yourselves fully to experience all the phases possible of sensuality and sexuality, in the bedroom and out. Don't expect to sow seeds today and harvest the crop tomorrow. Nature doesn't work that way. Sexual Repatterning doesn't either. Time is the magical quality, and what you do with that time makes the difference in whether or not you make your dream of love come true. Remember: love is the dream; *loving* is the reality.

We believe that couples whose chemistries match and who are capable of "nourishing" each other during their ups and downs can enjoy a deeply satisfying sexual-spiritual relationship.

To rekindle and recapture the glow, the excitement, of sensual sexual experience, a couple needs a suitable atmosphere, without the daily responsibilities and chores. A change of scene is helpful. If at all possible, plan to spend a weekend together, just the two of you, periodically; every six to eight weeks is about right. If you have children, this may take some doing. Perhaps the grandparents would take them for a weekend, and you can have your time together at home if it isn't possible to go somewhere else. Perhaps you could sleep (or make love) in another space for that weekend. One couple slept in the living room, another on their patio.

It may be difficult for some people to acknowledge, let alone accept, the need for this, and a weekend programed for "sex only" may be a minor disaster, like our own weekend we described earlier. As one woman expressed it, "Send the kids off for the weekend, and stay home and fuck! Are you out of your mind?" But think of such times as "mini-honeymoons," as times to try out new "things to do," in-bed things *and others too.*

Claude says: "The real benefits lie in the opportunity to be together, free from the usual routines, and in the kind of space where you feel easy about *whatever* you want to share. Then just go with it."

Dorothy says: "We think of these times as 'human intercourse,' times to share a book, a bit of verse. We take the time to talk about what really concerns us in life and living. Sometimes we just want to be quiet. Claude likes to sketch, we both like to walk. We enjoy exploring the area we have chosen. And our sexual expression can range from downright 'gutsy' to positively illuminating. We return home refreshed."

"Mini-honeymoons" represent perfect times to get in touch with those extended and expansive states of being that open the gateway for couples who want to grow together.

EXPERIMENTS

1. Awareness through Hands

Seat yourselves facing each other, nude.

The man extends his hands, palms up. The woman places her hands lightly, palms down, just in contact with his.

Concentrate on the backs of your hands until you can sense awareness there.

Transfer awareness to the palms; then to the space between—though there isn't much physical space.

Discuss what you experienced. Remember, there is no right answer. Whatever you did experience, even if it was "nothing," is what's important.

Repeat the experiment with the woman extending her palms upward and the man lightly placing his hands on hers.

Project your awareness into the palms of your partner. Continue until you have some sense of certainty, exchange roles, then discuss your experiences.

2. Energy from Hands

One partner places hands out, palms up. The other places hands, palms down, on the partner's hands and projects the concept of an energy flow from his or her hands to the partner's. Start the flow, and then stop it. This can be felt as tingling, warmth, prickling, or just "something."

Share what you are experiencing or not experiencing. Some people become aware, some don't.

3. Awareness Transfer via ESP

The room should be warm enough so that you will be comfortable lying on top of the bedclothes in the nude, side by side.

Whoever goes first mentally chooses a partner's body part, any body part, and concentrates awareness there.

The partner, who does not know what part has been chosen, is to project a feeling of "openness" to receive the message.

An attitude of acceptance by both partners that this transfer is possible will improve the results.

Discuss what each of you sensed.

Take turns doing this back and forth as long as you desire.

4. Genital Area Awareness

Choose a time when you both agree it is all right for there to be no orgasmic response during a sexual contact, which is to be of some duration.

Lie side by side, in a comfortable position, facing each other, with as much skin contact as possible. Take sufficient time really to sense this. Be aware of the space between your bodies.

Project your awareness onto that portion of the skin of your partner that is in contact with you.

When you have recognized this awareness—or if that doesn't come, when you feel you have done what you could—switch to the Von Urban position (see page 83).

After making entry, use no movement, or just enough to maintain the man's erection, if that is desired.

Be aware of your genitals; the man should be aware of his penis, the woman of her labia and vagina.

Continue this long enough to obtain whatever certainty you can.

Communicate together.

Reverse the process so that each becomes aware of the *other's* genitals.

Share your perceptions.

5. Energy Flow via the Genitals

Lie together as in Experiment 3, and consciously send energy into your partner's body. Use the genitals as the focal point. It may be helpful to *visualize*, in your mind's eye, a "stream" going from your body into the body of your mate. Share your experiences.

6. The Vital Presence

When you are close without sexual contact, try to develop your awareness of a radiant and vital "presence" between you. Allow yourself to experience this as fully as possible—both in bed and out.

16

From Now On

There is no way for us to know if you are newlyweds (young or older), if you've been divorced and remarried, if you are single, a couple, or engaged. Whatever your status may be, we hope that sharing our experiences has helped you to become aware of ways in which an ordinary couple *together* can achieve a meaningful, fulfilling relationship in every aspect of their lives.

All of us have been trussed up in centuries-old cultural agreements. Slowly, together, chapter by chapter, we have been snipping away at the bindings, freeing ourselves more and more, flexing long-unused physical and spiritual muscles, allowing various forms of awareness and experiencing to emerge—sensual, sexual, and spiritual.

Think back to how you felt about "you" at the beginning of the Sexual Repatterning process, and share your feelings. Look again at the questions in Chapter One. Are your answers the same as the ones you gave originally? Talk about what you have liked in the book, what you disliked. Reminisce about what you expected to find. Compare this with what you have gained.

With what you have learned as the base, you can go on to find for yourselves your own patterning with respect to sexuality, communication, and sharing. Refresh your memories from time to time with the main points:

Learn to see and appreciate your mate as she or he is.

Be realistic about your expectations.

Trust your senses.

Accept that you can *learn together* how to make love.

Understand *how* your bodies work.

Explore together to find better ways to develop your love skills.

Practice attuning yourself to the other's needs.

Understand your own sexual rhythm.

Use your imagination and fantasy in creative ways to aid the growth of your relationship.

Experiment to find new ways to grow.

Share your thoughts and feelings.

Emphasize what is *right* about yourselves before you consider what is wrong.

Stop *trying* and start *allowing* yourselves to experience together.

Respect the other's view.

Balance your resentments with your appreciations.

Put energy into creating what you *do* want instead of into what you *don't* want.

When in doubt, *communicate*, listen, hear, and understand the best you can!

Truly learn when and how to *shut up!*

Be as open and honest as you can.

Satisfy your curiosities and longings together.

Forgive your mistakes, but *learn* from them.

Let your mate think for himself or herself.

Share common goals and dreams.

Like each other and enjoy being together. Cultivate common interests and activities that allow for one another's needs.

Attune yourselves to the flow of life about you.

Take time each day to be quiet, to sense *your* part, your next step in your development.

Open wide the inner doors, and let out your sensitivity toward the seen and the unseen—the physical and the spiritual. We hope you will discover, as we have, that sexuality is the pathway to spirituality.

Glossary

Analingus   Caressing of the anus with the mouth

Anal Intercourse   Penis-anus intercourse

Anus   The external opening leading into the rectum

Aphrodisiac   A substance which, when consumed, causes sexual interest by engorgement of the genitalia

Autoeroticism   Masturbation

Cervix   The outlet of the uterus within the vagina

Climacteric   The change in sexual hormonal secretions, usually occurring in middle-age; in the woman, also called the menopause

Clitoris   A small sensitive organ at the upper part of the vulva, homologous to the penis of the male

Coccyx   The lower end of the spine, tail bone

Courtesan   A prostitute

Cunnilingus   Caressing of the vagina or vulva with the mouth

Digital   Manipulation with a finger or fingers

Fellatio   Mouth/penis intercourse

Flatus   Intestinal gas

Frenulum   A small fold of skin, specifically the fold on the lower surface of the glans of the penis

Glossary

Glans   The conical body that forms the outer end of the penis, or the clitoris

Labia Majora   The outer lips of the vagina

Labia Minora   The inner lips of the vagina

Masturbation   Stimulation of the genitals using organs other than genitals; usually manual (hand) stimulation

Oral-Genital   Caressing of the genitals (male or female) with the mouth

Perineum   That area of the crotch from the pubic arch to the coccyx

Pubic Bone   The front portion of the pelvis

Pubococcygeus   The muscle group extending from the pubic bone to the coccyx which provides support for the crotch area and sphincteric function for the anal, vaginal (in the female), and urethral openings

Scrotum   The pouch containing the testes

Seminal Vesicles   Small sacs in the ducts from the testes

Semen   The fluid produced by the male reproductive organs

Smegma   The waxy substance secreted by the sebaceous (fat) glands of the clitoris and labia minora in the female, or by the sebaceous glands of the prepuce (foreskin) in the male

Urethra   The tube for discharge of urine extending from the bladder to the external opening, the meatus

Vulva   The external genital organs of a woman

Bibliography

Bach, George R., and Deutsch, R. M. *Pairing.* New York: Peter H. Wyden, 1971.

Bartell, Gilbert D. *Group Sex.* New York: Peter H. Wyden, 1971.

Berzing, Bud. *Sex Songs of the Ancient Letts.* New York: University Books, 1969.

Breedlove, William, and Breedlove, Jerrye. *Swap Clubs.* Los Angeles: Sherbourne Press, 1964.

Bristol, Claude. *The Magic of Believing.* New York: Prentice-Hall, 1948.

Brusendorff, Ove, and Henninsen, Paul. *Love's Picture Book.* 4 vols. New York: Lyle Stuart, 1969.

Clark, LeMon. *101 Intimate Sexual Problems Answered.* New York: New American Library, 1968.

Cleugh, James. *Love Locked Out.* New York: Crown, 1964.

De Ropp, Robert S. *Sex Energy.* New York: Delacorte Press, 1969.

Deutsch, Ronald M. *The Key to Feminine Response in Marriage.* New York: Random House, 1968.

Dodson, Victor. *Auto-Erotic Acts and Devices.* Los Angeles: Medco Books, 1966.

Bibliography

Downing, George. *The Massage Book.* New York: Random House, 1972.

Edwardes, Allen. *The Jewel in the Lotus.* New York: Lancer Books, 1965.

———. *Erotica Judica.* New York: Julian Press, 1967.

Edwardes, Allen, and Masters, R. E. L. *The Cradle of Erotica.* New York: Julian Press, 1963.

Eichenlaub, John E. *The Marriage Art.* New York: Delacorte Press, 1967.

Ellis, Havelock. *Studies in the Psychology of Sex.* Philadelphia: F. A. Davis, 1900.

Fast, Julius. *What You Should Know about Human Sexual Response.* New York: G. P. Putnam's Sons, 1966.

Garrison, Omar. *Tantra: The Yoga of Sex.* New York: Julian Press, 1964.

Gillies, J. *My Needs, Your Needs, Our Needs.* Garden City: Doubleday, 1974.

Goldberg, B. Z. *The Sacred Fire.* New York: University Books, 1958.

Hagerman, R. J. *Oral Love.* Los Angeles: Medco Books, undated.

Harkel, Robert L. *The Picture Book of Sexual Love.* New York: Cybertype, 1969.

Intercourse (author unknown). City of Industry, California: Collectors Publication, 1968.

Jacobus, Dr. *L'Ethnologie du Sens Genitale.* 5 vols. Paris, 1935.

Karlins, M., and Andrew, L. *Biofeedback, Turning on the Power of Your Mind.* Philadelphia: Lippincott, 1972.

Kinsey, Alfred C., et al. *Sexual Behavior in the Human Male.* Philadelphia: W B. Saunders, 1948.

———. *Sexual Behavior in the Human Female.* Philadelphia: W. B. Saunders, 1953.

Knight, Richard P., and Wright, Thomas. *Sexual Symbology.* New York: Bell Publishing, 1957.

Koble, W. M., and Warren, R. *Sex in Marriage.* 2 vols. San Diego: Academy Press, 1970.

Kokken, Sha. *A Happier Sex Life.* Los Angeles: Sherbourne Press, 1966.

Lewinsohn, Richard. *A History of Sexual Customs.* New York: Harper & Row, 1957.

Marshall, D. S., and Sugges, R. C. *Human Sexual Behavior.* New York: Basic Books, 1971.

Masters, R. E. L. *Forbidden Sexual Behavior and Morality.* New York: Julian Press, 1966.

———. *Sex Driven People.* Los Angeles: Sherbourne Press, 1966.

———. *Sexual Self Stimulation.* Los Angeles: Sherbourne Press, 1967.

Masters, R. E. L., and Houston, Jean. *The Varieties of Psychedelic Experience.* New York: Holt, Rinehart & Winston, 1966.

Masters, William H., and Johnson, V. E. *Human Sexual Response.* Boston: Little, Brown, 1966.

Montagu, Ashley. *Touching.* New York: Columbia University Press, 1971.

O'Reilly, Edward. *Sexercises Isometric and Isotonic.* New York: Crown, 1967.

Oriental Love (author unknown). New York: Cybertype, 1969.

Perls, Frederick; Hefferline, R. F.; and Goodman, P. *Gestalt Therapy.* New York: Dell, 1965.

Petronius. *Satyricon.* New York: Mentor Books, 1959.

Ploss, H. H.; Bartels, B.; and Bartels, P. *Femina Libido Sexualis.* New York: Medical Press, 1965.

Reik, Theodor. *Myth and Guilt.* London: Hutchinson, 1958.

Rosebury, Theodor. *Life On Man.* New York: Viking, 1969.

Bibliography

Schutz, William C. *Here Comes Everybody.* New York: Harper & Row, 1971.

Shostrum, Everett, and Kavanaugh, James. *Between Man and Woman.* Los Angeles: Nash Publishing, 1971.

Stern, Bernard. *Medizin, Aberglaube und Geschlecsleben in Derturkei.* 2 vols. Berlin, 1933.

Tart, C. T. *Altered States of Consciousness.* Garden City: Doubleday (Anchor), 1972.

Traube, Ray. *Sex Fun and Games.* New York: Belmont, 1968.

Van de Velde, T. H. *Ideal Marriage.* New York: Covici-Friede, 1937.

Vatsyayana. *The Kama Sutra.* New York: Capricorn Books, 1963.

Von Urban, Rudolf. *Sex Perfection and Marital Happiness.* New York: Dial Press, 1949.

Wang, Shih-cheng. *Love Pagoda.* North Hollywood: Brandon House, 1965. (Introduction by Albert Ellis.)

Wedeck, Harry E. *Dictionary of Aphrodisiacs.* New York: Philosophical Library, 1961.

Wells, John. *Tricks of the Trade.* New York: Information, Inc., 1970.